EXPLORING FORT VANCOUVER

Exploring
FORT VANCOUVER

EDITED BY

Douglas C. Wilson & Theresa E. Langford

FORT VANCOUVER NATIONAL TRUST
VANCOUVER, WASHINGTON

in association with

UNIVERSITY OF WASHINGTON PRESS
SEATTLE AND LONDON

FORT VANCOUVER NATIONAL TRUST
General O.O. Howard House, 750 Anderson Street
Vancouver, WA 98661, USA
www.fortvan.org

UNIVERSITY OF WASHINGTON PRESS
PO Box 50096, Seattle, WA 98145, USA
www.washington.edu/uwpress

LIBRARY OF CONGRESS CATALOGING-IN-PUBLICATION DATA
Exploring Fort Vancouver /
edited by Douglas C. Wilson and Theresa E. Langford. — 1st ed.
p. cm.
ISBN 978-0-295-99158-0 (pbk. : alk paper)
1. Fort Vancouver National Historic Site (Wash.)—Antiquities.
I. Wilson, Douglas Calvin. II. Langford, Theresa E.
F899.V2E96 2011
979.7—dc22   2011012415

The paper used in this publication is acid-free and meets the minimum requirements of American National Standard for Information Sciences—Permanence of Paper for Printed Library Materials, ANSI Z39.48.1984.

P. II: *The Chief Factor's House with evergreen Christmas decorations on the verandah.* Courtesy of the National Park Service.
P. IV: *Fort Vancouver National Historic Site with Mount Hood in the background.* Courtesy of the National Park Service. Photo by Tracy Fortmann.
P. VI: *The side gate of the reconstructed fur trading post.* Courtesy of the National Park Service.
P. XVIII: *A modern rendition of Fort Vancouver showing its extensive garden and orchard.* Courtesy of the National Park Service.

CONTENTS

ACKNOWLEDGMENTS

THE GENESIS OF THIS BOOK occurred during planning for the 60th anniversary of archaeology at Fort Vancouver in 2007. From that germ of an idea, many have contributed time, effort, and expertise to this project. The authors would like to especially acknowledge Stephanie Toothman, Associate Director for Cultural Resources for the National Park Service; David Louter, Pacific West Region Chief of Cultural Resources; and Diane Nicholson, Pacific West Regional Curator, who continue to throw their support behind a strong cultural resources stewardship program at Fort Vancouver tied to other parks and partners.

Archaeological Laboratory Director Elaine Dorset provided editorial and image assistance and, along with graduate students Elizabeth Horton, Dana Holschuh, Meredith Mullaley, Stephanie Simmons, Janna Tuck, Katie Wynia, and Dianna Woolsey, continues to provide motivation for ongoing archaeological studies at the site. We are particularly indebted to the students of the Public Archaeology and Public History field schools, students of Dr. Wilson's Historical Archaeology, Cultural Resources Management, and Field Methods in Archaeology classes, and to our colleagues at Portland State University, Washington State University Vancouver, and the Center for Columbia River History, particularly Ken Ames, Virginia Butler, Steve Weber, Bill Lang, Candice Goucher, Katy Barber, and Donna Sinclair.

This project would not have been possible without the support and enthusiasm of the Fort Vancouver National Trust. Since 2003, the Trust's Board of Trustees, led by Ed Lynch and Bing Sheldon, and staff, led by President and Chief Executive Officer Elson Strahan, have been strong supporters of the historical archaeology field school and have provided support for educational and interpretation programs. In addition to these leaders, we would like to thank Chief Operations Officer and Chief Financial Officer Mike True and Communications Manager Susan Parrish who sought grants, in-kind contributions, and have made the Trust co-publishers of this book. Susan, in particular, provided unflagging support for the project, working closely with the authors, copy editors, designer and others to ensure that the educational product prepared by the National Park Service was transformed into a beautiful book.

Special thanks are also due to the Clark County Historical Promotion Grant Program, a grant from which ensured publication of this book and will allow free copies to be distributed to area schools and libraries.

And, most of all, to the many people who have graced this extraordinary place—the indigenous peoples from over 30 Indian tribes, Native Hawaiians, Canadians, Chinese, African Americans, English, Scots, Russians, American citizens, archaeologists, historians, landscape architects, historical architects, and curators. All have contributed to the unique story of Fort Vancouver both in the past and today.

ABOUT THE AUTHORS

DR. DOUGLAS C. WILSON is Director of the Northwest Cultural Resources Institute, Archaeologist for the Pacific West Region of the National Park Service, and Adjunct Associate Professor of Anthropology at Portland State University. He received his Ph.D. in Anthropology from the University of Arizona in 1991.

THERESA E. LANGFORD is Curator for the Northwest Cultural Resources Institute, Fort Vancouver National Historic Site, and Lewis and Clark National Historical Park. She received her Master's Degree in Applied Anthropology from Oregon State University in 2000, and a graduate certificate in Collections Care from George Washington University in 2006.

DR. ROBERT J. CROMWELL is Archaeologist for the Northwest Cultural Resources Institute and Fort Vancouver National Historic Site. He received his Ph.D. in Anthropology from Syracuse University in 2006.

HEIDI K. PIERSON is a Museum Specialist who oversees the McLoughlin House Unit of Fort Vancouver National Historic Site. She received her Master's Degree in Anthropology from California State University in 2008.

GREGORY P. SHINE is Chief Ranger and Historian for Fort Vancouver National Historic Site, Historian for the Northwest Cultural Resources Institute, and Adjunct Faculty in the Department of History at Portland State University. He received his Master's Degree in U.S. History from San Francisco State University in 2000.

TRACY A. FORTMANN is Superintendent of Fort Vancouver National Historic Site. She received her Master's Degree in Political Science from Arkansas State University in 1982. Tracy was named the 2001 and 2008 Superintendent of the Year for Cultural Resources Stewardship for the Pacific West Region of the National Park Service, and she was the regional recipient of the 2008 Appleman-Judd-Lewis Award for Cultural Resources Management.

FOREWORD

YOU ARE HOLDING a treasure in your hands. There are beautiful artifacts illustrated here from the Fort Vancouver collections, but this is more than a picture book. The authors—all experts in the history of Fort Vancouver—share their fascination with history so you will find the artifacts pleasing to the mind as well as the eye. There are no better people to tell the story than these individuals, who have dedicated their careers to this place.

There is a human need to make both emotional and intellectual connections with stories and objects from the past. We respond to both beauty and puzzles. We rely on wonder and fascination to lead us to discovery, and discovery is the heart of archaeology.

Modern archaeologists are fond of the saying: "It's not what we find, it's what we find out." We say that because we are dedicated to discovering the historical meaning of artifacts, and sometimes the aesthetics of objects can distract and cause passionate collectors to forget that the work must be done meticulously, recording the archaeological context in great detail. Archaeology, of course, is also about what we find, and at Fort Vancouver, six decades of research have resulted in collections of international renown.

Archaeology requires a love of discovery, which takes place when something is found not only in the soil but also in the lab and the archive. Discovery happens through the process of research, when the "mystery" artifact is identified, when clues to answering a long-standing question are found, or when something unexpected makes us ask new questions.

Many of Fort Vancouver's collections are the result of archaeology, and the findings that allow the accurate reconstructions of the fort today also are archaeological. The place itself is a treasure: from ongoing excavations to the garden to the palisade to the buildings to the new Land Bridge, its pieces are symbolic of so many connections and so many journeys.

Far more substantial than "avatars" and the virtual reality of such modern phenomena as the online game "Second Life," Fort Vancouver allows us to walk through an actual place. While you are there, allow yourself to imagine being in a different set of circumstances. Look into the past to open your mind to others' experiences.

Find yourself and your own story in this book. Perhaps you are new to the state of Washington or to the United States; many of the people who left their mark on Fort Vancouver were also newcomers. All across the globe, people have been swept up in two centuries of mind-boggling change. Fort Vancouver's residents and passers-by lived that change as you are living today's sweeping changes. Their story is your story. Find your connections to Fort Vancouver.

◈ Barbara J. Little
Archaeologist, National Park Service, Washington, DC
Editor, *Public Benefits of Archaeology*
Author, *Historical Archaeology: Why the Past Matters*

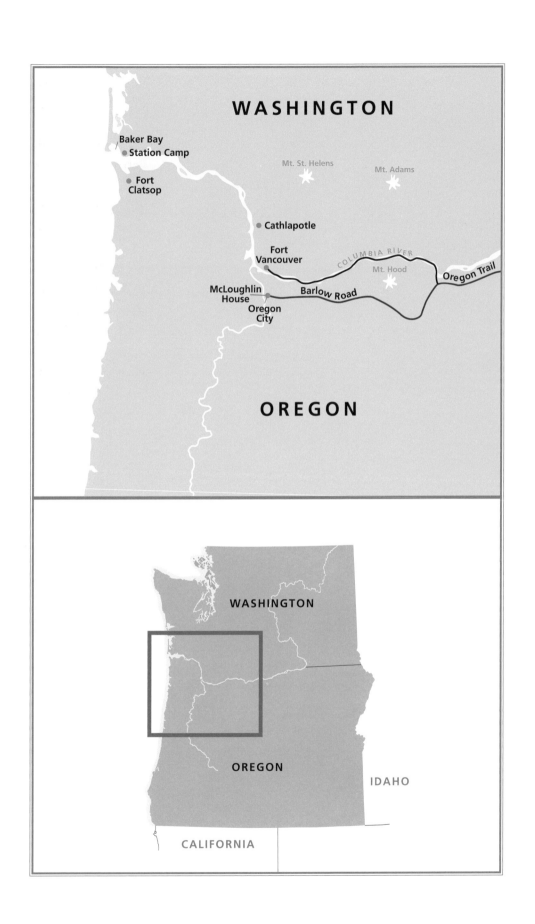

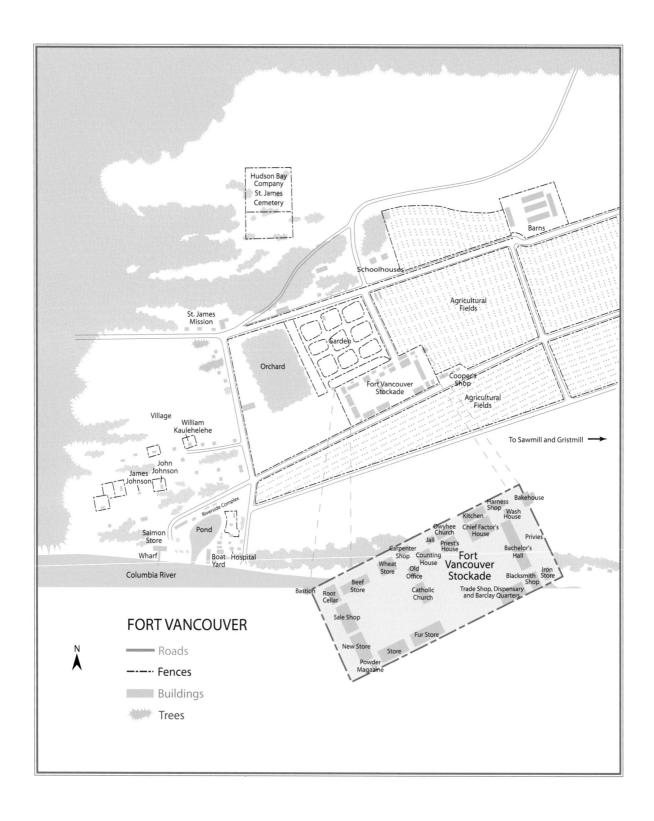

FORT VANCOUVER

Hudson Bay Company St. James Cemetery

Barns

Schoolhouses

St. James Mission

Orchard

Garden

Agricultural Fields

Fort Vancouver Stockade

Cooper's Shop

Agricultural Fields

Village

William Kaulehelehe

To Sawmill and Gristmill →

John Johnson

James Johnson

Riverside Complex

Salmon Store

Pond

Wharf

Boat Yard

Hospital

Columbia River

Bastion

Root Cellar

Beef Store

Sale Shop

New Store

Store

Powder Magazine

Carpenter Shop

Wheat Store

Old Office

Counting House

Catholic Church

Fur Store

Owyhee Church

Jail

Priest's House

Kitchen

Harness Shop

Chief Factor's House

Wash House

Bakehouse

Privies

Bachelor's Hall

Fort Vancouver Stockade

Blacksmith Shop

Iron Store

Trade Shop, Dispensary and Barclay Quarters

Roads

Fences

Buildings

Trees

N

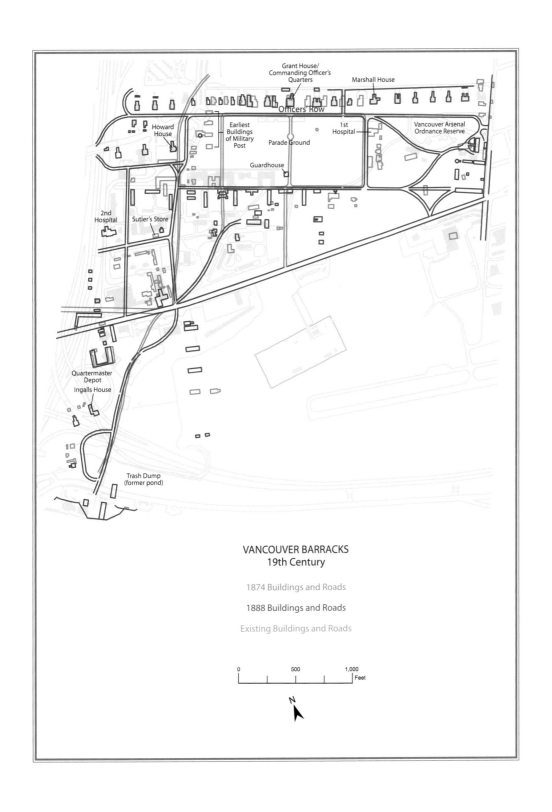

Grant House/
Commanding Officer's
Quarters

Marshall House

Officers' Row

Howard
House

Earliest
Buildings
of Military
Post

Parade Ground

1st
Hospital

Vancouver Arsenal
Ordnance Reserve

Guardhouse

2nd
Hospital

Sutler's Store

Quartermaster
Depot

Ingalls House

Trash Dump
(former pond)

VANCOUVER BARRACKS
19th Century

1874 Buildings and Roads

1888 Buildings and Roads

Existing Buildings and Roads

0   500   1,000
                         Feet

N

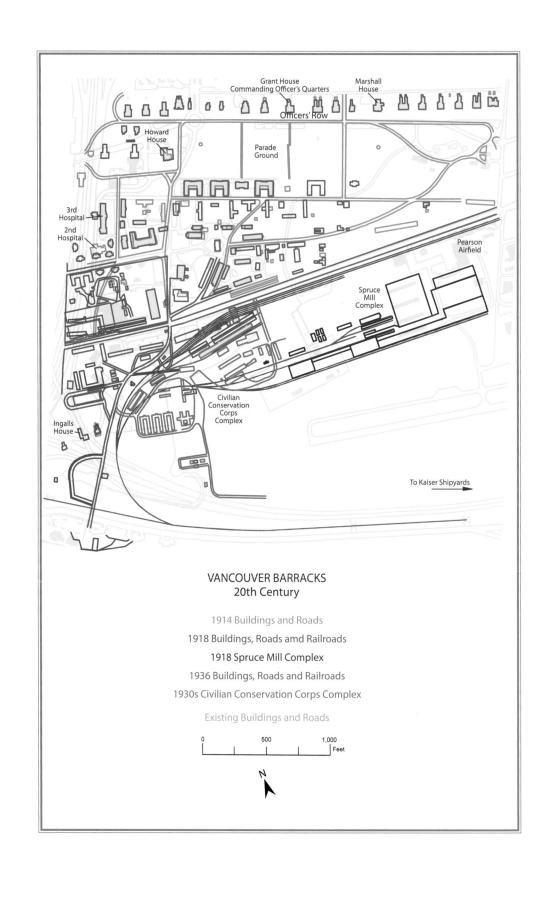

Grant House
Commanding Officer's Quarters

Marshall
House

Officers' Row

Howard
House

Parade
Ground

3rd
Hospital

2nd
Hospital

Pearson
Airfield

Spruce
Mill
Complex

Civilian
Conservation
Corps
Complex

Ingalls
House

To Kaiser Shipyards

VANCOUVER BARRACKS
20th Century

1914 Buildings and Roads

1918 Buildings, Roads amd Railroads

1918 Spruce Mill Complex

1936 Buildings, Roads and Railroads

1930s Civilian Conservation Corps Complex

Existing Buildings and Roads

0   500   1,000
                         Feet

N

EXPLORING FORT VANCOUVER

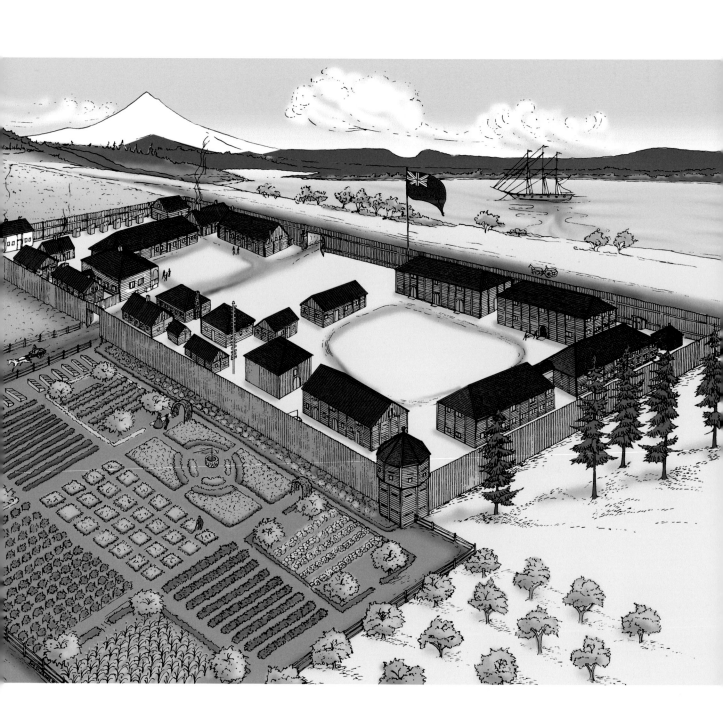

FORT VANCOUVER

History, Archaeology, and the
Transformation of the Pacific Northwest

◆ *Douglas C. Wilson*

AT FORT VANCOUVER, the landscape is dominant. The Columbia River's influence is evident everywhere, from the distinctive ancient terraces, remnants of great floods, to the gravelly silt that forms the soil beneath one's feet. From the vantage of the Visitor Center, on the northeastern margins of the park, the land slopes off the terrace to the south, to the plain that fronts the wide river. From this plain, at the reconstructed fort, evergreen-covered mountains and hills edge the horizon. On a clear day, Mt. Hood punctuates the western skyline, with its volcanic bulges and snowy sides and peak, the dark bands of the Cascade Mountains falling about around it. Other volcanoes can be seen from certain vantage points, including Mt. Jefferson to the south and Mt. Adams to the east. Pointed tops of fir and hemlock line Harney Heights to the east and, farther away, the Portland West Hills to the south and west. Together, these mountains and hills form a skyline today that has not changed significantly for tens of thousands of years.

A thousand years or more ago, the plain was an open, level prairie, with oaks, grasslands, and swampy wetlands and ponds. Some oaks are still present as isolated, great trees, or as small groves interspersed between army barracks. A gallery of trees, including cottonwoods and willows grew along the bank of the river. Animals, including deer, elk, bear, and coyote roamed the plain. Salmon, steelhead, sturgeon, and

The Vancouver Land Bridge commemorates the Native people who lived near the Columbia River before Lewis and Clark's expedition. The art and educational features of the installation, designed by famed architects John Paul Jones and Maya Lin, explore the changes that have occurred on the lower Columbia River over the past two centuries.
Courtesy of the National Park Service. Photo by Roman Len.

other fish were abundant in the river, and birds, both migratory and permanent, flocked and nested in trees on the plain.

The landscape today is a visible reference to the resources which brought people here, starting thousands of years ago. The mountains and forests formed barriers, but were also rich in timber, minerals, animals, and other plants. The prairie was a source of wild tubers, grasses, and game animals, and later a convenient place to grow crops. The river, far from a boundary, was both source of fish and a canoe, boat, and ship highway that provided access to the fur-bearing animals of the interior—the richest resource that first brought Europeans and Americans to this country.

One can envision the first people coming to this place, Indians with conical basket hats, finely carved canoes, and cedar plank houses; or the first Europeans and Americans, dressed in buckskin and elk hides, or in Victorian attire, with beaver hats, cravats, and waistcoats; or the first soldiers in pre-Civil War uniforms, with rifled muskets, cannon, and all the accoutrements of war.

Fort Vancouver's history documents the tremendous changes that have taken place in the Pacific Northwest, and the world, over the past two hundred years. Beneath the ground lie the physical remains of that amazing history, traces of its most famous occupants and visitors, and the legacy of the many different people from around the world who have worked, played, celebrated, mourned, worshiped, and called this place home. This book illustrates some of the more evocative museum objects that are tied to this landscape. Researchers have recovered many of these artifacts from archaeological excavations, starting in 1947 and continuing today. Individuals have donated some of the objects—items carefully passed down from person to person, generation to generation. All of the items, whether they were unearthed through archaeology or donated to the park, are kept at the park's museum collection facility, where National Park Service curators and museum specialists care for over two million objects.

The story told by these artifacts is one of dramatic transition—from a society dominated by stone, basketry, wood, and bone to a colonial frontier society dominated by iron, ceramics, and glass, whose major endeavor was the extraction of natural resources from the land and water. From there, the trajectory of change led steeply to a global society, dominated by plastic goods, that is now one of the wealthiest and most powerful nations on earth. The artifacts within this book speak to this transformation. The emergence of the modern Pacific Northwest is cluttered with the legacy of its transmutation, one that is both beautiful and terrible. Learning from past objects is highly rewarding, as archaeology and history peel away the layers of time to reveal the passages of our society, the context of the past, and the heritage of the present. These things even hint at future possibilities.

HISTORY'S CENTRAL PLACE IN THE PACIFIC NORTHWEST

In 1805, when Meriwether Lewis and William Clark floated past the small prairie on the edge of the Columbia River, where Fort Vancouver would be built, they were sitting in their own dugout canoes and carried flintlock muskets to feed and protect themselves. The indigenous people, ancestors of today's Chinook, Cowlitz, Grand Ronde, Warm Springs, and Yakama, also used hand-carved canoes and for thousands of years had depended on stone, wood, and bone tools and weapons. William Clark first described the people of the basin of the Columbia River where Portland, Oregon, and Vancouver, Washington, are now situated:

> On the Main Lard ["larboard" or southern] Shore a Short distance below the last Island we landed at a village of 25 Houses: 24 of those houses we[re] thatched with Straw, and covered with bark, the other House is built of boards in the form of those above, except that it is above ground and about 50 feet in length and covered with broad Split boards This village contains about 200 men of the Skil-loot nation I counted 52 canoes on the bank in front of this village maney of them verry large and raised in bow.

The soldiers, guides, and other members of the Corps of Discovery led by Lewis and Clark ate wapato, given to them by local native people, for the first time at this village. Wapato is the Arrowhead plant (*Sagitaria latifolia*), a tuber that grows in wetland areas along the margins of the Columbia River and elsewhere throughout North America. It was one of the favored foods of indigenous people (and of the Corps of Discovery, once they tasted it). While the foods, houses, and people of the lower Columbia River impressed the explorers, they also saw familiar items. As they traveled through the area, Lewis and Clark noted some of the first representatives of foreign products that would soon dominate in the colonial period: "Scarlet & blue blankets Salors jackets, overalls, Shirts and Hats," a sword, copper and brass trinkets, beads, "Muskets or pistols, and tin flasks to hold their powder," copper kettles, and other items of non-native manufacture. Already, by 1805, the European world of goods had made an impression on the people of the lower Columbia River.

The indigenous people of the Northwest were among the most complex hunter-gatherer societies in the world. Cultural Anthropologists Robert Boyd and Yvonne Hayda have estimated that in the Portland/ Vancouver Basin, the resident population of approximately four to five thousand Chinookan people would swell to nearly ten thousand

Wapato (Sagitaria latifolia) was a staple for the pre-contact and contact-period American Indians of the lower Columbia River. A form of Sagitaria is used for food in China and Japan today and is cultivated in the San Francisco Bay Area for Asian markets.
Courtesy of Melissa Darby.

during the spring run of salmon. Far removed from the stereotypical image of migratory bands of hunters portrayed in the modern media, these people lived in villages of hundreds, perhaps even thousands, of individuals. Many lived in one place most, or all, of the year, producing large amounts of processed and stored foods, building large plank houses that held from thirty to one hundred people each, and actively improving prairie habitats through burning to provide better growth of berries, roots, and forage for deer, elk, and other game animals. As described by Kenneth Ames and Herbert Maschner, in *Peoples of the Northwest Coast: Their Archaeology and Prehistory*, the indigenous people of the lower Columbia River practiced a well-defined and distinctive art form and maintained a stratified society with hereditary leadership positions. There were also conflict and slavery as well as clear concepts of wealth and status. Impressive, carved canoes facilitated regional transportation, including that undertaken for trading and warfare. The items traded over the greatest distance were probably obsidian from central Oregon and marine shells from the Pacific Coast.

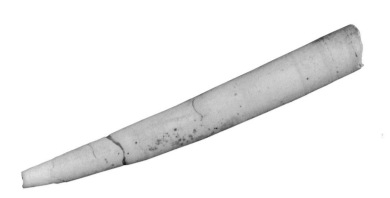

Two important trade items of pre-contact American Indians: Obsidian (right, FOVA 21849, 2.3 cm L), traded from central and eastern Oregon, and dentalium (left, FOVA 173368, 3.5 cm L × .4 cm D), traded from the Pacific coast.

The Fur Trade

As documented by Lewis and Clark, European goods quickly permeated the indigenous cultures of the lower Columbia River in the early nineteenth century. Sailing ships loaded with products from Europe and Asia, having traveled thousands of miles from England and New England around the tip of South America, would anchor at Baker Bay at the mouth of the Columbia River. Members of the Chinook, Clatsop, and other local groups would trade otter, beaver, and other animal pelts for glass beads, metal knives and axes, copper and brass trinkets, muskets, gunpowder, and other items. By the time Lewis and Clark wintered at Fort Clatsop, over one hundred ships may have ventured to the Pacific Northwest, with at least thirteen visiting the mouth of the Columbia. After Lewis and Clark, fur traders from the United States and Canada began setting up more permanent fur trading posts. The North West Company, a British fur trading business, established Spokane House in 1810, near modern Spokane, Washington. In 1811, the Pacific Fur Company, an enterprise of John Jacob Astor of New York, founded Fort Astoria at the mouth of the Columbia River within the current boundaries of Astoria, Oregon. Astor's agents sold Fort Astoria to the North West Company in 1813, giving the North West

Company a nearly monopolistic control over the region's fur resources. The post was renamed Fort George in honor of King George III.

This early trade brought fundamental changes to the lives of local native people. European firearms, diseases, and alcohol had profound impacts on health and affected indigenous warfare and slavery. Artifacts found at Chinookan villages along the Lower Columbia River, such as the Meier and Cathlapotle sites excavated by Portland State University under the direction of Kenneth Ames, have recorded the introduction of fur trade items into long-inhabited villages. At the McGowan/Station Camp site, near Baker Bay, excavations by the National Park Service and Portland State University document the changes the fur trade brought to Chinookan culture. Archaeologists found an abundance of fur trade items amongst the remnants of traditional plank structures identified with the Lower Chinook's Middle Village. Items included gunflints, musket balls, imported fine English creamware pottery, Chinese porcelain ceramics, trade knives, glass beads, clay tobacco pipes, and jewelry. These products introduced new patterns in consumption that were tied to personal and household status, the acquisition of natural resources, and economic and trade relationships between tribal groups.

The Fur Trading Post

The relationship between indigenous people and fur traders throughout the Pacific Northwest changed further in 1821 when the North West Company merged with the Hudson's Bay Company. In 1825, to improve the prospects of the Company's Columbia Department operations, Governor George Simpson and Chief Factor John McLoughlin established Fort Vancouver within the boundaries of what is now Vancouver, Washington. This post became the core of the Hudson's Bay Company's western operations, essentially controlling the fur business from Russian Alaska to Mexican California and from the Rocky Mountains to the Pacific Ocean, a territory of approximately 700,000 square miles. It was the principal settlement, port, factory, courthouse, and emporium for the Pacific Northwest, administering two dozen subsidiary posts and business undertakings throughout the region. During the 1830s and early 1840s, it was one of the largest colonial

Copper pendants from the Station Camp site, part of Lewis & Clark National Historical Park. Copper items, whether imported as finished pieces or fashioned locally from reused copper kettles and other forms, were highly valued among the people of the Columbia River. (Left: FOVA Lot 1514, Spec 1; 6.21 cm L. Right: FOVA Lot 2590, Spec 1; 3.07 cm L.)

settlements in the Pacific Northwest, dwarfing Mexican Yerba Buena, California (the precursor to San Francisco), and rivaling Russian New Archangel, Alaska (Sitka).

In its wooden stockade, bastion with cannons, and log buildings, the establishment of Fort Vancouver is symbolic of the spreading frontier development of the Pacific Northwest. It was unique in both the scope of its economic enterprise and its multicultural community. The fort acted as a supply depot that distributed goods to other trading posts and collected furs for transport to England. Because of its remoteness, the uncertainty of supply from Europe and the east, and the natural resources in the area, Chief Factor McLoughlin initiated a variety of industries, including logging, ship-building, and farming, to support and diversify the economic pursuits of the Company. These activities produced food and other products to supply employees and to sell to the Russians in Alaska, Hawaiians in Hawaii, and American missionaries and other immigrants who began coming to the Pacific Northwest in the 1830s. At its height in 1845, Fort Vancouver was the nexus of a corporate farm that contained over 1,200 acres under cultivation, nearly 2,000 head of cattle, 2,000 sheep, 1,500 hogs, 700 horses, an orchard, a seven-acre formal garden, a lumber mill, a gristmill, a salmon packing operation, boat-building facilities, a hospital, schoolhouses, and a Roman Catholic mission. It was the principal supplier of European-manufactured goods to employees at the fort and the other far-flung posts of the Company. It also served the missionaries and American

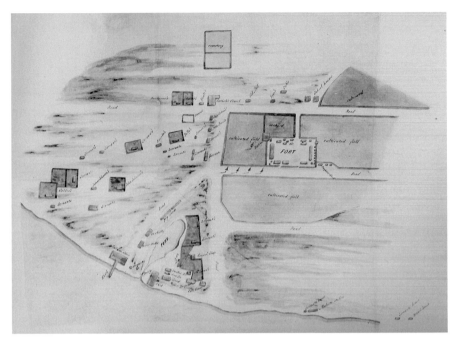

Fort Vancouver, ca. 1845, by Richard Covington. Courtesy of the Washington State Historical Society.

settlers who, beginning in the 1840s, flooded over the Oregon Trail into the Willamette Valley. From its stores, Fort Vancouver supplied the people who started the great transitions of population, technology, and culture of the Pacific Northwest.

Fort Vancouver was the first terminus of the Oregon Trail. The many accounts by missionaries, explorers, and traders illustrated McLoughlin's success at agriculture and other commercial pursuits. His accomplishments encouraged Americans to settle in the Pacific Northwest. The first travelers across the Oregon Trail used the Columbia River as a route to the trail's end at Fort Vancouver. When Samuel Barlow blazed his road across Mt. Hood, Oregon City on the Willamette River, became the trail's primary terminus, 26.5 miles upstream from the Columbia, but McLoughlin preserved the influence of the Hudson's Bay Company through improvements, including a gristmill, sawmill, and retail store that served the burgeoning immigrant communities. McLoughlin's influence and benevolence to the pioneers is reflected in his modern title as the "Father of Oregon." While he proffered credit to destitute Oregon Trail immigrants, he also made a healthy profit as the primary supplier of commercial goods.

As such, Fort Vancouver bore the early fruits of the Industrial

The people who lived at Fort Vancouver included Americans, English, French-Canadians, Hawaiians, Irish, Métis, Portuguese, Scots (including Shetland and Orkney Islanders), and Indian tribes from across the continent whose historic designations included Cascades, Californian, Carrier, Cayuse, Chaudières, Chehalis, Chinook, Clallam, Cowichan, Cowlitz, Cree, Delaware, Grande Dalles, Haida, Iroquois, Kalapuya, Kalama, Kathlamet, Kholtl, Klickitat, Mollala, Mowatwos, Nez Perce, Nipissing, Nisqually, Okanagan, Pend d'Oreille, Rogue, Shasta, Snake, Snohomish, Spokane, Stikine, Tillamook, Tsnoomus, Umpqua, and Walla Walla.

Revolution and then distributed them throughout the Pacific Northwest. Many of the items manufactured at or imported to the fort are the last vestiges of ancient European technologies, some of which date to the medieval period or before. Others are representative of the flood of new materials and product forms that were being manufactured in English factories near the end of the 1700s. These items, such as transferprinted ceramics, machine-manufactured nails, and factory-made textiles, were transforming the world of commerce by the time Fort Vancouver was established. In these objects, these offspring of the Age of Enlightenment, we can see the roots of technological and social changes that altered the ways houses were built, food was delivered to homes and presented on tables, and otherwise affected and directed lifestyles.

The Fort's Village

Fort Vancouver was home to a surprising diversity of people. The factors that led to this diversity are part historical coincidence and part geography, including the merging of two great and far-flung fur trading companies, the limitations of mid nineteenth-century transportation, and the resident indigenous populations of the Pacific Northwest. The merging of the Hudson's Bay Company and the North West Company involved a synthesis of two already distinct sets of people. Scots, Englishmen, and their North American descendants generally formed the upper echelons of the hierarchy, including the clerks, Chief Traders, and Chief Factors. Since its origins in the seventeenth century, the Hudson's Bay Company had typically hired people from northernmost Scotland, especially the Orkney Islands but also the Shetland Islands and the Hebrides, and company workers traded, interacted, and often intermarried with Cree and other people of the Hudson Bay area. The North West Company customarily employed French-Canadians, Iroquois, and other Indians as laborers, trappers, voyageurs, and hunters. The Canadian fur trade resulted in an entirely new cultural group that also became a part of the vibrant Fort Vancouver community. The offspring of European and white American fur traders and native women created a new identity—the Métis, who reshaped elements of both American Indian/First Nation and European/American cultures

into a new culture. The Hudson's Bay Company brought together these diverse groups of people at Fort Vancouver.

The remoteness of the Pacific Northwest required ships from the ports of England or the eastern seaboard of North America to sail around the tip of South America to reach the region. Hawaii was a natural stopping place for vessels on the way to the Pacific Northwest. Because of this, and the attractiveness of foreign employment for Hawaiians, the Company employed large numbers of Hawaiians as sailors and laborers; and by the 1850s, the village at Fort Vancouver was known as Kanaka Village or Kanaka Town by American settlers. Kanaka means, among other things, "human being" in Hawaiian. The Hudson's Bay Company also maintained a ship-based maritime fur trade that sailed along the coastlines, headquartered at Fort Vancouver. Through this trade, sailors from around the world were introduced to the mix of people who lived in the new community.

Even before the fur trade, the density of distinctive indigenous

The early U.S. military and Hudson's Bay Company forts, ca. 1855, by Gustavus Sohon. The Hudson's Bay Company fort is to the right (south) with the north end of the Village in the foreground, while the U.S. Army fort is to the left (north), with the sutler's palisaded store and the Catholic mission in the foreground. Courtesy of the National Park Service.

groups and languages along the Columbia River was one of the highest in the world. The integration of the fur trade with local populations led to an unprecedented mixture of people, languages, and industries, all within the community that sprouted near the warehouses and fields of Fort Vancouver. These people worked in a class-conscious and economically stratified British corporate system. They drove the machinery, plows, and ships of Fort Vancouver, and they lived, formed families, and died within the shadows of its walls. The artifacts found at Fort Vancouver and the remains of their houses and gardens represent the ways they forged new lives during this period of intense contact and economic, technological, and social change in this region.

The Army Fort

In 1846, the United States and Great Britain signed a treaty that set the international boundary at the forty-ninth parallel. Three years later, the U.S. Army established its first fort in the new American territory, on the prairie above the Hudson's Bay Company post. This garrison, which held the departmental headquarters, quartermaster's depot, and arsenal for the military, was also called Fort Vancouver until 1879 when it was renamed Vancouver Barracks. The post formed the nexus of military operations in the Pacific Northwest and was central to conflicts with Indians and the active development of infrastructure for the new territory, especially road building. The U.S. military's Fort Vancouver formed a cultural center that pushed out more traditional worlds and embraced American ideals and products.

This new Fort Vancouver would serve as a proving ground for many of the nineteenth and twentieth centuries' most important military and civilian leaders. Numerous Civil War generals suffered the hardships of the frontier post at Vancouver prior to their service (to both the North and South) in the Civil War. After the war, many military leaders used Fort Vancouver as place of advancement through the service. Fort Vancouver has been host to some of the most notable people in the history of the United States, including generals, surgeons, engineers, and presidents. This post, so remote from the power and influence of Washington, D.C., undoubtedly helped mold the character of these soldiers. Shared experiences at Fort Vancouver, including

Quarters of Gen. Grant in Ft. Vancouver - Wn -   P125-BV

adversity, camaraderie, and trials under fire, formed one of the cru-cibles in which leaders were forged.

Like the Hudson's Bay Company post, the early U.S. military fort was simple in character. The Army built its earliest quarters of logs and heated them with wood-burning fireplaces and stoves. Kitchens were detached structures, and the soldiers used outdoor toilets called privies or sinks. Refuse was discarded casually behind barracks and kitchens. One of the structures from this earliest post still survives. The Commanding Officer's Quarters, at the heart of Officers' Row, is called the Grant House today in honor of Ulysses S. Grant, who came to Vancouver as a Brevet Captain in the Quartermaster Corps. While he never lived at the house named in his honor, the Vancouver, Washington community recognized his importance to the nation and the region when he visited the post after his presidency. The resident of the house when Captain Grant was at Fort Vancouver was Lieutenant Colonel Benjamin L. E. de Bonneville, an important U.S. explorer and famous soldier in his own right.

Within fifty years, the post became a bastion of Victorian culture, reflecting the material styles of the era as well as dramatic innovations in military, domestic, and other technologies. Accompanying this

The Commanding Officer's Quarters at Fort Vancouver (Vancouver Barracks), now called the Grant House. Courtesy of the National Park Service.

The Howard House, home of Oliver Otis Howard and other commanders of the Department of the Columbia and Fort Vancouver/Vancouver Barracks. Courtesy of the National Park Service.

transition were fundamental changes in post and community planning as well as in health and sanitation. Of considerable importance to the history of the post, the U.S. Army reorganized in 1878, with one new requirement—that military officers stay on government property with their troops. This resulted in the construction of a fine Italianate-style house for the Commander of the Department of the Columbia, General Oliver Otis Howard, a Civil War veteran who headed the Freedman's Bureau after the war (1865–1872), helped found Howard University, and fought in the Nez Perce War of 1877.

Like many soldiers of the Civil War and the Indian Wars, Howard was a complex and sometimes contradictory person. While he was known as the "Christian General" and is a central figure in the elevation of African Americans through his post–Civil War work, he also commanded the United States' troops in the subjugation of the Nez Perce Indians. Later, after the Nez Perce War, he advocated on the tribe's behalf.

During the 1880s, Victorian buildings sprouted along Officers' Row, supplanting the old log structures. The most impressive of these is the Queen Anne–style home now known as the Marshall House, after its most famous twentieth-century occupant, General George C. Marshall. In 1886, when the house was constructed, General John

Gibbon was its resident. Like Grant and Howard, Gibbon was a Civil War soldier. He led the famed Iron Brigade and served on the Surrender Commission at Appomattox Courthouse. He also was in charge of the force that relieved the besieged Captains Reno and Benteen at Little Big Horn in 1876, and he led U.S. troops against the Nez Perce at the Battle of the Big Hole in 1877. From 1936 to 1938, the house was the quarters for General Marshall, who was commander of the post, and for the Depression-era Civilian Conservation Corps regional head-quarters. Marshall became the U.S. Army Chief of Staff during World War II, then Secretary of Defense and Secretary of State. He headed the American Red Cross and received the Nobel Peace Prize in 1953 for developing the Marshall Plan, which helped rebuild post-war Europe.

The Marshall House, first inhabited by General John Gibbon, and later by George C. Marshall. Courtesy of the National Park Service.

The barracks for the soldiers changed as well, from simple log struc-tures to frame structures, to those designed on standardized plans in the 1880s and 1890s. After the Spanish-American War (1898), the post expanded to include large barracks with central heating, hot water showers, flush toilets, and large windows to let in light and air.

Like the Hudson's Bay Company employees, the nineteenth-century military was diverse in character. According to the 1850 census, the soldiers at Fort Vancouver included Germans, Irish, English, Scottish,

French, and Canadian immigrants. Chinese sojourners worked for officers and soldiers at the post. These ethnic Chinese, primarily from Guangdong and Fujian provinces in southeastern China, came to the western United States to make their fortunes. In 1899, Company B of the Twenty-fourth Infantry Regiment, an African American "Buffalo Soldier" outfit, arrived at Fort Vancouver after exemplary service on San Juan heights during the Spanish-American War.

During the nineteenth century, women were also a substantial part of the military community. Besides the wives of officers who likely strove to maintain the Victorian ideal of domesticity, Irish and American laundresses were present on the post and worked for the Army. Laundresses were one of the few occupations in the Victorian era that permitted a woman to earn a living and support her family. Laundresses could supplement their income through selling food or alcohol or by offering midwifery services to women in the surrounding military or civilian communities. An industrious laundress could make much more money than an army private.

A sutler—a civilian contractor, usually attached to a specific post—provided goods to the soldiers of the garrison. In the earliest years of the military fort, the sutler competed with the Hudson's Bay Company's retail business, supplying goods to the burgeoning settlement of Vancouver and its surrounding farms. In 1880, the first post canteen in the nation was created at the site, leading to the formation of the post exchange (PX) system still used in the military today.

During the twentieth century, the post continued to transform itself in response to the rapidly changing world and the development of the Pacific Northwest. One of the most dramatic changes to the landscape occurred in response to the April 1917 entry of the United States into World War I. Military leaders believed aircraft provided one means of breaking the stalemate of trench warfare in France. The wood and fabric aircraft construction of the time relied on light, strong wood; and aircraft manufacturers highly prized the Pacific Northwest's Sitka spruce trees. To meet the Army's wartime order of 100 million board feet of aircraft-quality spruce, and to resolve a labor strike by the Industrial Workers of the World, the U.S. Army, under Colonel Brice Disque, nationalized the timber industry. Army troops of the Spruce

A Section of
THE WORLDS LARGEST SPRUCE "CUT-UP" PLANT, VANCOUVER BKS. WASH. 1918.

Production Division, headquartered at Vancouver Barracks, worked at logging camps and lumber mills throughout the Pacific Northwest. Disque formed a new labor organization, the Loyal Legion of Loggers and Lumbermen (known as the 4 L) and instituted labor reforms—an eight-hour workday, sanitary living conditions, and decent food.

The Spruce Production Division built an immense, specialized mill at Vancouver that employed three thousand civilians and soldiers. Prior to the armistice in November 1918, the maximum monthly production of the three shifts at the mill was 28 million board feet. Huge amounts of fill, drainage features, concrete foundations, and refuse dumps were laid down in the short period of its operation. These remains speak to the immense influence of the United States government on the outcome of World War I and to this critical point in the history of logging in the Pacific Northwest. The auction of equipment to civilians after the war offered four hundred steam-powered yarders, eighteen locomotives, and three hundred motor trucks. Further, the labor reforms and conditions at logging camps and mills that the government imposed continued in commercial logging operations after the war.

Like the spruce mill, the Depression-era (1933–1942) Civilian Conservation Corps (CCC) had a profound impact on the barracks. While the spruce mill lay roughly on top of the old Hudson's Bay Company stockade and surrounding gardens, orchards, and agricultural fields, the Army built its CCC headquarters on the site of the old village.

The spruce mill at Vancouver Barracks, on the site of the Hudson's Bay Company's Fort Vancouver. The tents are temporary dwellings for the thousands of soldiers employed in the mill. Courtesy of the National Archives and Records Administration.

Valery Chkalov's ANT-25, on the first transpolar flight, landed at Pearson Field.
Courtesy of Dale Denny.

The CCC provided young men jobs building roads, planting trees, and performing other activities in national forests and other public lands. Some structures and many remnants of the headquarters, barracks, roads, and infrastructure of the CCC post remain. Some of these speak to the nature of impermanent housing for the young men of the CCC, while some represent new ideas in promoting public hygiene, shared work experience, and the promotion of a national identity.

Another important part of the twentieth-century story of Vancouver Barracks is the development of early aviation in the Pacific Northwest. One hundred years after Lewis and Clark's 1805 expedition paddled past the site in dugout canoes, Lincoln Beachey floated high above and across the Columbia River in a dirigible. His 1905 flight from Portland to the Barracks was one of the first controlled flights in the United States. Other experimental aircraft used the polo grounds at the Barracks as a landing field. The Army Air Corps created the Vancouver Barracks Aerodrome in 1923, and later named it Pearson Field after one of the Army's most skilled pilots, Lieutenant Alexander

Pearson, Jr. Notably, in 1937, during General Marshall's tenure, Valery Chkalov and his crew completed the first transpolar flight in a single-engine ANT-25, landing at Pearson Field.

During World War II, the post served as training and administrative headquarters for the U.S. Army. The large Kaiser Shipyards, directly adjacent to the post, made Liberty Ships, LST landing craft, and "Baby Flat Top" aircraft carriers. The region's population swelled with workers, representing a new round of intense growth for the Pacific Northwest and continuing the dramatic demographic and cultural changes that epitomize the history of the area.

A National Park Service ranger interpreting at historical Well #2 within the Fort Vancouver stockade, in about 1950. Courtesy of the National Park Service.

Legacy and the Living Park

The remains of this impressive history are literally layered across the landscape. Artifacts, foundations, heritage trees, and surviving structures are the legacy of two centuries of change. The recognition of this history with the creation of the national park and the Vancouver National Historic Reserve is impressive as well. In 1915,

The McLoughlin House in Oregon City, a unit of Fort Vancouver National Historic Site, is one of the earliest preserved historic houses in the West. Courtesy of the McLoughlin Memorial Association.

the War Department identified the site of the Hudson's Bay Company Fort Vancouver as a National Monument under the Antiquities Act. While technically overstepping its authority to make such a designation, the Secretary of War's proclamation indicates the high degree of historical significance ascribed to the post at this time. Even after the World War I spruce mill added a new layer of fill on top of the old fur trading post, local and national interest in the site continued. After World War II, in 1948, Fort Vancouver became a part of the National Park System and was designated a National Historic Site in 1961.

In 1996, Congress authorized the Vancouver National Historic Reserve as a partnership between the City of Vancouver, the National Park Service, the U.S. Army, and the State of Washington. The Fort Vancouver National Trust is the lead nonprofit organization working closely with all partners. The historic district includes the national park and properties associated with the U.S. Army and the Hudson's Bay Company. In 2003, Congress added Oregon City's McLoughlin House Unit to Fort Vancouver National Historic Site. This unit preserves the

Louis Caywood excavating at Fort Vancouver in about 1947. Courtesy of the National Park Service.

houses of two of Oregon's early leading citizens, John McLoughlin and Forbes Barclay. Congress had designated the McLoughlin and Barclay Houses as a National Historic Site in 1941, and the McLoughlin Memorial Association managed them under a cooperative agreement. The Association has actively worked to preserve the houses since 1909 and is one of the earliest historic preservation organizations in the West.

Over the lengthy history of the park, there have been extensive archaeological excavations, reconstruction of buildings and landscapes, and development of historical programs and community events. The site's preservation, interpretation, and educational activities represent the newest layer of activities at this internationally significant place.

Most of the artifacts illustrated in this book represent the preserved legacy recovered by National Park Service, academic, and avocational archaeologists. Some of the earliest historical archaeology in the nation was conducted at Fort Vancouver. Louis Caywood, a student of Byron Cummings at the University of Arizona, started excavations for the National Park Service in 1947, one year prior to the site's inclusion in the National Park System. He continued excavation at the site for a number of years and produced a report of his work in 1955, discussing the nature of his finds and the remains of the structures he had discovered. After working at Fort Vancouver, Caywood joined National Park Service Archaeologist John Cotter at Jamestown and participated in the excavations at that early English settlement. Since then, many archaeologists have taken up Caywood's mantle at Fort Vancouver. These scientific explorers have left their own legacy in the form of carefully written field notes, drawings, photographs, catalogs, and analyses of finds. The years of dedicated effort allow us to see the dramatic changes in technology, transportation, health, sanitation, and culture that have occurred through time and are reflected in the objects highlighted in this book.

ARCHAEOLOGY

Archaeology is the study of people through the scientific examination of ruins and abandoned sites and their related artifacts, architecture, and other features. Archaeologists often survey sites by examining the finds discovered on the ground's surface, mapping architectural remains, and noting aspects of vegetation and topography that provide clues to the age of the site, its purpose, and the cultures that created and modified it. Sometimes, archaeologists dig into these sites to take samples of artifacts, learn about the different layers, or strata, that are present, and better understand their contents and research potential. These excavations can be minimal—simple tests into the site—or they can be extensive, trying to uncover the foundations of an entire building or to collect a large sample of artifacts from a particular location. Archaeologists usually dig in squares that are set on a grid. As archaeologists are scientists, they measure things systematically and take detailed notes on how they conducted their research, what they found, and where exactly they found it; and they itemize all their finds. Archaeologists do not loot sites. They conduct their research using carefully developed questions and for carefully considered goals. Because the artifacts themselves only tell part of the story, archaeologists spend a lot of time determining the provenience, or exact locations and associations, of finds. This can tell them how people made, used, and discarded their artifacts and can provide clues about how they lived. Because a site's context is so important and because digging destroys that context, archaeologists usually prefer to leave much of a site untouched, leaving future work to scientists who will have more advanced technology. Archaeologists believe that looting by artifact hunters, for sale or for their own personal collection, is objectionable. There are local, state, and federal laws that support the point of view that archaeological sites are national treasures. In Washington and Oregon, for example, it is illegal to loot any archaeological site on federal, state, and private lands. If a site must be disturbed, then an archaeologist must conduct research under a permit and with a specific, scientific research design.

Artifacts

As defined by archaeologists, an artifact is anything manufactured or otherwise altered by human hands. Artifacts include, for example, tools, manufacturing and maintenance by-products, fragments of pottery, bottles, shreds of fabric, and the like. While the word *artifact* is usually applied to those items studied by archaeologists and found on archaeological sites, we extend its definition in our collection to complete objects, antiques, photographs, documents, and everything traditionally classified as museum objects. Artifacts are not limited to old things, either. Cultures continue to manufacture, use, and discard artifacts. Thinking about our own, modern artifacts helps us understand past artifacts and their significance.

In American culture, like other consumer societies, our possessions surround us. Advertising wraps us in its silken, cocoon-like grasp, cheerfully telling us about the newest items in fashion, communications, cars, and toys. Bright, multicolored packaging, product logos, advertising jingles, "branding," friendly salespeople, and celebrity spokespeople persuade us of the desirability of all those new things, from breakfast cereals to pocketknives, cellular telephones to the latest cartoon-character toy. We are clothed in our artifacts, drive them around, display them as status symbols, and build them—our

homes—larger and more impressive than the neighbor's next door. As we strive to stay current and new, things that were once new are abandoned or lost. In our consumer-driven, material-rich world, we hardly notice their passage. Our material metamorphosis is the shedding of old things in quest of the new.

We sometimes encounter a thing that was made long ago—an object, or artifact, that was lost, abandoned, discarded, or perhaps passed down through generations. It may be complete and still functional, as it was when people first made it, or it may be aged and worn. In some cases, its dirt-encrusted and broken condition may speak of years of burial in the earth. Artifacts from the past make us wonder about how far we have come—individually, as a nation, as a people, even as a species. How much has changed since people first made and used it? An artifact can evoke the depth of our history, allowing us to reflect on the past through questions about the people associated with it. How different are we from the people who knew and used this thing, who desired it, depended on it, and eventually put it aside? What kind of people used it? Did they have a family? Did they worry about their children? Was their boss a good one? Did they struggle to bring a team together to accomplish a goal? Were they discriminated against? Did they enjoy recreation? Were they concerned about their health?

Artifacts provide a tie to people in the past, people who shaped, held, polished, admired, loved, used, repaired, and eventually discarded them. They can be objects of great beauty, like a china dish or a finely carved shell brooch; symbols of anger or violence, such as a bullet or an arrowhead; or objects of devotion, such as a crucifix.

Archaeologists seek to study the links between artifacts, past events, and people to understand people and their history. Historical archaeologists examine artifacts and compare the information that can be gleaned from them with documents of the time, such as diaries, maps, lists, and accounts. In a sense, archaeologists simply conduct a scientific and historical extension of what everyone does when they first see an object from long ago. We try to make sense of the past through these tangible things.

INTRODUCING THE COLLECTIONS

Each chapter in this book describes aspects of the history of Fort Vancouver through the lens of artifacts in the museum collection. Most of the artifacts were collected from the site through archaeological excavations. Some were donated to the park but are directly tied to the events and people associated with it. They represent some of the highlights of the Fort Vancouver collection. Each section uses these artifacts to tell the story of cultural and technological transitions that occurred at Fort Vancouver over the past two hundred years.

Identity explores the diversity of the frontier fur trade post and U.S. military fort. Artifacts can reflect differences and even actively participate in shaping cultural identities related to ethnicity, nationality, gender, and occupation. This process of "fitting in" and "standing out" is crucial in understanding the relations among cultural groups and within families in the Pacific Northwest. Curator Theresa Langford discusses how artifacts reflect the changing story of the people of the site.

Technology, introduced by archaeologist Robert Cromwell, explores the transition from medieval to modern at Fort Vancouver, examining how people in the Pacific Northwest transitioned from a stone tool society to a modern one in just two hundred years. The unique manner in which technological change came about in the Pacific Northwest, and at Fort Vancouver, is a fascinating story of innovations, marketing, resource exploitation, and the relationship of all of these to culture.

Museum Technician Heidi Pierson—in *Globalization* and *Health*—explores two unique aspects of people's lives. *Globalization* explores the linkages between the Pacific Northwest and the rest of the world through artifacts and styles that reflect faraway places and new mechanisms of trade, nationalism, and industrialization. The early and continuing connectedness of the Pacific Northwest with other places, including the Pacific Islands, Asia, and Europe, has helped form the character of the region. The importance of global trade in the development of the area is reflected in the artifacts found at Fort Vancouver.

The recurring experience of epidemics, the role of addictive drugs, the diet of settlers and soldiers, and the tools to fight disease are fundamental aspects of Pacific Northwest history and have formed the identity of the region. The *Health* section explores changes in medical theory, sanitation, and diet as they are reflected in the remains of medicines, foods, and other items. These things tell us much about the changing nature of human experience in the West.

The Park Today, by Chief Ranger and Historian Gregory P. Shine, explores how modern-day interpreters, scientists, and park rangers use the material legacy of the site in reaching out to visitors. The link between collections, archaeology, and the history of the site presents both challenges and opportunities in engaging the public with the history of the Pacific Northwest.

The final section, *Why Collections Matter*, by Superintendent Tracy Fortmann, discusses how the modern park, including the museum collection, continues to influence our own history. Understanding this extraordinary place and its legacy—as seen in artifacts, historical structures, reconstructed buildings, and exhibits—continues to shape current events and guide new leaders.

The promise and possibilities of Fort Vancouver are of great significance to everyone who lives in or visits the Pacific Northwest. I hope you will find that the treasures of Fort Vancouver are not just the tangible pieces of the past but that their true value is in the dawning of understanding and the transformation of perspective. In short, I hope you will better realize the significance of the past and the intimate connections between historic sites, artifacts, history, and the shape and direction of our future. Through recognizing an artifact's significance in history, we might better understand our place and role in society. Through seeing our place in our world more clearly, we improve that world and leave a lasting legacy for future generations.

The diverse people who have inhabited this place, their changing views of society, and the transformations over the past two hundred years are the subjects of this book. I encourage you to make your own connections between artifacts and people, the past and the present, and the origins and development of the American Pacific Northwest.

IDENTITY

Using Objects to "Fit In" and "Stand Out"

◈ *Theresa E. Langford*

THOSE THINGS WITH WHICH WE SURROUND OURSELVES—
the clothes and jewelry we wear, the furniture we sit on, the toys we
play with—have for millennia helped us express our sense of self and
our place in society. The tie between one's personal belongings and
one's identity is a close and enduring one. Artifacts excavated from an
archaeological site, even hundreds or thousands of years after their
use, can give us an idea of an individual's religious beliefs, political
leanings, economic class, or cultural traditions. Historic objects with
good context can help characterize someone no longer living.

Identity is a fluid concept with overlapping meanings. We define
ourselves as individuals, we define ourselves as members of groups,
and others define us (as an individual or as a group) from an outside
perspective. Objects can reflect and reaffirm these different identities
and their sometimes complementary or contradictory natures. They
may be used to declare loyalty to a group or ideal or, conversely, to
stand in opposition to an established order or assumed expectation.
In addition, common, everyday objects may be used in creative ways
to illustrate distinction from others.

Within the world of the fur trade, identity was inextricably linked to
ethnicity and occupation in a self-perpetuating system in which each
element served to reinforce the others. The Hudson's Bay Company's
chain of trading posts, stretching across the continent, was a British

political and economic structure that imposed its hierarchy on a multicultural population of employees and their families. An early version of what has been termed "corporate colonialism" in modern times, the Hudson's Bay Company was both business and governing body in the absence of any formal regime. As reiterated by Susan Lawrence and Nick Shepherd, "colonialism is best understood as a material phenomenon linked to the circulation of new sets of material culture and practices." Although categorization for each individual within this system was somewhat fluid and advancement based on merit was possible though uncommon, general trends of prejudice were more than evident.

Male employees were divided into two ranks. The "gentlemen"—Chief Factors, Chief Traders, clerks, etc.—were generally English, Scottish, or French-Canadian. The engagés—tradesmen, trappers, voyageurs, laborers, and the like—were usually French-Canadian, American Indian, Hawaiian, or Métis, a term denoting mixed European and Native heritage. This class duality remained in effect throughout the decades of the fur trade, resulting in a stratified society in which status, salary, and prospects for change were generally dictated by one's cultural background.

A woman's identity was inextricably tied to that of her male partner. Compared to the diverse employees, the female population was more homogeneous, being mainly Métis or natives of tribes who lived near the trading post. Many were married *à la façon du pays*, or "in the fashion of the country." These alliances, arranged outside the jurisdiction of a church, could be life-long, faithful unions or transitory connections. Although their labor was critical to the success of posts and brigades, women were rarely officially employed by the Company. Their identity within the fur trade system depended on association with a father or husband. This dependence left women vulnerable, but it also, in a sense, gave them more flexibility to create or change their identity. It was not one cemented at birth, but one that could evolve over a lifetime.

When individuals joined a fur company, often leaving their homelands far behind, their beliefs and traditions modified in response to new environments, different types of people, and long periods of time away from the influences of their native cultures. Trappers and voyageurs, the brigade guides, particularly professed a preference for a "life of freedom" outside the pressures of society. The fur trade had grown to become a separate way of life, with its own cultural symbols and traditions.

Fort Vancouver was a microcosm of the larger fur trade culture, a post where even the physical arrangement reproduced class differences and preferences. As described by Peter Nelson:

> Fort Vancouver was a place where structures were ordered according to their symbolic importance from its earliest existence...at Fort Vancouver, there was a definite distinction between the different types of structures based on the status of the person who dwelt or worked there. The higher status structures were separated from others through visual signals or symbols and the non-verbal communication inherent in their construction style and maintenance.

Despite the parameters of the built environment, it was also a world in which people could use objects to maintain identities they accepted or admired and to resist identities they resented. The entire population wore British-style clothing (at least three years out of fashion) and purchased mass-produced European goods for their households. Luxury items such as decorated china dishes, jewelry, and domestic knickknacks became social equalizers, symbols of status that all could display. At the same time that people in the village were using these types of objects to appear British, they were also using modified trade goods and traditional materials to maintain a cultural identity separate from that of the Company elite.

There were, of course, other indicators of identity: the location of one's house, the language one spoke, the color of one's skin. But objects, like no other symbol, could be *chosen*. They functioned as mobile expressions of one's identity. A vast array of goods—from imported European and Asian items to local, traditionally made ones—were at people's fingertips in the Sale Shop, and buyers wholeheartedly embraced the opportunity to pick and choose.

Fort Vancouver was also a scene of rapidly shifting identities, as individuals responded to the pressures of assimilation, proselytizing by missionaries, and the demise of the fur trade. Accepted practices within fur trade culture were soon challenged by American settlers emigrating over the Oregon Trail, bringing with them more conservative values from the East. For the first time, the people of Fort Vancouver faced intense criticism of certain aspects of their lifestyle, including unsanctified unions and marriage between people of different ethnicities. Missionaries—mainly Roman Catholic, Anglican, and Methodist—had expressed similar concerns and had seen some success in converting and changing behaviors. Many of them had also modified their expectations to incorporate fur trade lifestyles. Immense numbers of immigrants from the East meant that the face of the region and the identity of its earlier inhabitants were forever altered. In 1846, the boundary between the United States and Canada was finally set at the forty-ninth parallel (where it remains today). This decision, a watershed moment for the Oregon Country, meant that Fort Vancouver operated on foreign soil and would soon be under an American provisional government.

In tandem with these pressures, the Northwest fur trade began to destroy itself. The Company's "fur desert" policy—leaving few live animals for competing companies to harvest—had exterminated so many animals that large-scale trade could not be sustained. The Company moved its headquarters from Fort Vancouver to Fort Victoria, British Columbia. Employees of the Company, the vast majority of whom were British citizens, faced an unenviable crossroads and an uncertain future. Many retired to farm or homestead, while some stayed near Vancouver and adapted their identities to the new political and social system. Others retreated to Indian reservations, Canada, or other homelands.

With the arrival of the U.S. Army, a slow change in the material culture began. Different suppliers, different technologies, and different preferences on the part of purchasers are reflected in the types and styles of objects remaining from this time period. Nevertheless, these objects were utilized as symbols of identity in ways identical to their predecessors. Just as the occupants of Fort Vancouver and the village used objects to express their identity, so too did the officers, enlisted men, and families at Vancouver Barracks. Social stratification, ethnic variability, political and religious differences—all the assumed characteristics and beliefs that form our identity—are symbolized by the objects they left behind.

Similar to the fur trade, the Army was a structured world where officers, generally from the eastern United States, commanded a corps of culturally diverse troops; separation of the classes was strictly enforced. And, just like the neighboring fur trading post, the physical layout of Vancouver Barracks served to reinforce separation between officers and enlisted men by segregating their dwellings, messes, and privies. Not only this, but the design took advantage of the gently sloping site to place officers' houses and offices literally above the troops' barracks. Despite being a frontier station, Vancouver mirrored the discipline, rank, and emphasis on order of any other military post, utilizing naturally occurring topography to underpin these ideas.

Class differences were buttressed by the restricted material goods available to enlisted men and laundresses. Until the late nineteenth century, the Army awarded sales commissions to civilian retailers, one per post, known as sutlers. One of Vancouver's first sutlers was Elijah Camp, who arrived in 1852 and ran a profitable business for several years until, as reported by Ulysses S. Grant in a letter to his wife, his store was mysteriously "blown up." Despite the ominous start, the sutlery tradition continued, eventually evolving into the Army's first post canteen—the beginning of the global Army and Air Force Exchange System—in 1898. Camp's customers would have browsed amid a limited array of items, supplements to their government-issue goods, which could be consumed or stored in spartan quarters. Officers and their families, with more wealth and connections at their disposal, had more latitude in placing personal orders and bringing belongings along as they moved from post to post; these freedoms are reflected in the wider range of materials they left in the archaeological record.

The material remains of Vancouver Barracks often speak of classification, a world where identity was bound with rank and assignment. But they also remind us of the sometimes overlooked inhabitants: the women, children, and civilians living at the post. Even within a sphere that could discourage individualism, all found ways to express their sense of self in the objects they acquired, and subsequently lost.

The rule of written history is that all but a few are forgotten. The vast majority of people who were once on earth are no longer in our collective records. Individuals who were illiterate or of lower social standing, women, children, ethnic minorities—all these groups, and more, are often represented solely by the physical remnants of their lives. Material culture can help fill the resulting gaps in our knowledge. The importance of using collection items to comprehend the range of people represented at this site, to bolster their place and roles in history, cannot be overstated.

It is an irony of studying the past in this way that we can often understand people, can discover intimate details about their lives, without ever knowing exactly who they were. The connections between a tangible object and its symbolic meanings, and the "true" identity of its owner, have been severed. The emotional power of museum items often lies not in their association with a famous person but in the fact that they are not sterile objects. Each of them passed through a person's hands, touched his or her body or heart, and took on meaning because of that contact. Pieces of our identity are captured in the objects we leave behind. Our possessions form our biography.

PIPE

Within recent centuries, political statements in figurative form have appeared on many types of everyday items, including chamber pots, tea cups and saucers, and smoking pipes. In the late nineteenth century, potent Irish symbols began to appear on British-made goods marketed to Irish immigrants in America. Not only are these types of goods especially significant among recent immigrants who have a particular need for reminders of their heritage, but the material culture also assists in creating a new identity for the diaspora. The items become group identity in tangible form, commercially available.

This tobacco pipe is one such artifact. It was manufactured in Scotland; the design supports Irish nationalism with its text, harp, and shamrocks; and it was imported to the Oregon Country. It was excavated from the area of the former village pond, which had served as a dump site for the U.S. Army post; the soil layer in which it was found was deposited prior to a flood in 1887. The owner is unknown but was possibly an enlisted soldier in the diverse corps stationed at Vancouver Barracks or a laundress attached to the post. In that decade, a significant percentage of the troops were Irish, many of them very recent immigrants. It is likely that the smoker was a supporter of the "Home Rule" movement of the 1880s, which was designed to win more self-governance for Ireland. Use of the pipe would have expressed this political sentiment to any witness and reaffirmed an identity with every inhalation.

Pipe
FOVA 21700 (4.6 CM H × 3.8 CM DIAM.)

Crucifix
FOVA 15262 (44.63 mm H ×
26.24 mm W × 3.3 mm DIAM.)

Rosary
FOVA 10362 (Beads: .5 cm DIAM.;
Average height of medals: 2 cm H)

CRUCIFIX, ROSARY, MEDAL, & BEAD

Religious observances were an integral part of life at Fort Vancouver, and several belief systems coexisted. Company employees were Roman Catholic, Anglican, Protestant, or sometimes Methodist, though Catholicism was the most common faith at the post. Usually at least two types of services were offered each Sunday to meet the needs of whomever wanted to attend. In the 1830s, Church of England Reverend Beaver and his wife made a brief stay at the post and vociferously denounced fur trade marriages contracted without the participation of clergy. Beaver wrote: "Private houses on the outside of the Fort, should be provided for the former unhallowed purposes, nor should women, so living [outside of Christian marriage], be permitted to take any part in the management of domestic affairs of the establishment, beyond the confines of their own families." Catholic missionaries arrived soon after Beaver's departure, in response to a request by the Company's French-Canadian and Métis employees that had been forwarded to headquarters by John McLoughlin. The priests established St. James

Mission, first inside the fort walls within an old warehouse building and later just to the northwest of the fur trading post. William Kaulehelehe and his wife were brought in from the Islands to provide spiritual guidance to the Hawaiian workers, and he held services inside the fort, at the building known as the Owyhee Church.

The first service at Fort Vancouver presided over by Catholic priests was on November 27, 1838, and included "evening prayer, made in common, a pious reading was made and some sacred songs were sung in French." Francis Blanchet, later the first Catholic bishop of the Oregon Territory, wrote: "These meetings became so attractive as to draw, on many occasions, the Bourgeois, clerks and their families to enjoy the pleasant and harmonious concerts. The Indians themselves did not remain insensible to the charms of these chants, nor were they the last to come and hear them in large number, sometimes 70 and 100." Tension between Catholic and Protestant religions in the Oregon Country is reflected in Blanchet's belief that the delay in obtaining

Bead
FOVA 157875 (20.89 L × 10.09 DIAM.)

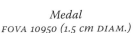

Medal
FOVA 10950 (1.5 CM DIAM.)

permission from the Hudson's Bay Company for the Catholics to establish a mission was due to the presence "in the country [of] Anglican, Methodist and Presbyterian ministers." He wrote: "the difference in teaching might create dissentions among the Indians; for this reason and perhaps to give them time to proselyte, the grant of passage was withdrawn [in 1837]." Conflict between the religions for the "souls" of the Indians and colonial settlers continued throughout the nineteenth century.

For Catholics, religious identity could be made obvious by wearing a crucifix, rosary, or religious medal like those shown here. These types of artifacts are rarely recovered from Fort Vancouver, despite the prevalence of Catholicism among Hudson's Bay Company employees. The scarcity of religious items in the site's archaeological record perhaps reflects the care with which individuals kept track of these types of belongings. This crucifix was found near village dwellings belonging to John and James Johnson. The site was excavated in the early 1980s and yielded the second largest collection of Hudson's Bay Company domestic artifacts in the Northwest (surpassed only by the nearby Chief Factor's House).

The brass and wood rosary was recovered in the 1970s from the Bachelors' Quarters privy inside Fort Vancouver. Despite its name, the Bachelors' Quarters building was a string of small, connected apartments inhabited by the Company's junior officers and their families. The privy, besides functioning as an outhouse, was also a general trash pit. The rosary was in a layer whose deposition has been dated to between 1841 and 1850 and is thought to represent the debris of one or more families.

Production of this type of religious medal, which seems to be a variation of the Miraculous Medal and shows the Virgin Mary with the words *Qui avons recours à vousor*, "Who have recourse to thee," began in 1832. It was found within the area of the fort stockade, near the site of the Iron Store.

The blue glass bead is believed to have come from a rosary and includes a Tree of Life design molded into its surface; it was recovered near the site of the St. James Mission.

Thimble
FOVA 15246 (2 cm H × 1.7 cm DIAM.)

Coin
FOVA 131180 (2.2 cm DIAM.)

THIMBLE & COIN

A hallmark of fur trade culture that is often re-flected in archaeological remains is the creative use of utilitarian items. Sewing thimbles, a simple tool in European and American society, evolved into a favorite decorative object in Indian and Métis cultures. At Fort Vancouver, the quintessential brass thimbles are almost always recovered with a purposeful perfora-tion in the top, enabling them to be hung from bags or clothing, or incorporated into neck-laces. Prior to the founding of Fort Vancouver, George Simpson reported that a "made beaver" pelt would purchase two-dozen brass thimbles at Fort George (Astoria). In the spring of 1844, there were over 7,400 thimbles in stock at Fort Vancouver. The thimble pictured here was found in the village area, near the John and James Johnson homes, and likely reflects the multiethnic heritage of their households. Both men lived with Indian women, and their per-sonal goods would have merged European and indigenous preferences.

Coins, too, are often found with holes drilled into one edge so they could be re-cycled as personal adornment. Currency was rare in the Oregon Country; most transac-tions were based on credit or, after the 1849 California gold rush, gold. Coins were enough of an anomaly that they were attractive not as legal tender but as ornaments. This American quarter was manufactured in 1834. It, too, was recovered from the village area. Though it was found near the military's Quartermaster's Ranch, it likely predates that complex and is associated with an earlier village house of the Fort Vancouver community. Thimbles and coins (as well as beads) are symbols of the syn-cretic nature of the fur trade way of life; people wholeheartedly adopted objects from more dominant cultures but adapted them for new uses in their own lives.

TUMBLER, BULLET, & PISTOL (CONTINUED ON NEXT PAGE)

Archaeology is about patterns. A site is largely interpreted by analyzing how artifacts are distributed, the frequencies with which they occur, and their spatial relationships. It is rare that a single object can be tied to a known individual. This tumbler is one of the wonderful exceptions. Adolphus Lee Lewes (also spelled Lewis), the owner who scratched his name on the bottom, was a clerk and surveyor employed at Fort Vancouver from 1840 to 1845. Lewes drew the first plat map of Oregon City in 1844. He settled the first claim on the Lewis River at Woodland, Washington, but he later returned to service at Fort Vancouver. By marking his possessions (four of these tumblers were found strewn about near the Bachelors' Quarters or in the building's privy), Lewes assured that his identity would be forever captured in the glass. The fact that he did so, however, leaves us with more questions than answers. Why, for example, did he feel so possessive about an everyday drinking glass, something his company would have provided, and why were several broken around the same time? It's a frustrating puzzle, answers to which could provide insight into not only the everyday workings of Fort Vancouver, but also the man who left these objects behind.

Though this pistol, like the tumbler, can be traced to an individual owner, the objects' similarity ends there. The routes they took in coming to the museum collection are as opposite as they could possibly be. Both of these items were important enough to their owners that they were marked with a personal name, but over time one became "trash" and one became an "heirloom." The pistol was the personal sidearm of General Oliver Otis Howard, a Civil War veteran who was commander of the Department of the Columbia during the 1870s and based at Vancouver Barracks. When donated by his descendant, the pistol was accompanied by a bullet, reputedly one that wounded Howard at the Battle of Fair Oaks in 1862 and caused the amputation of his arm. At that time, Howard was a brigadier general in George B. McClellan's Army of the Potomac. Howard later wrote about the incident in his autobiography:

Tumbler
FOVA 10435
(3.7 cm H × 7 cm BASE)

Bullet
recent acquisition
(1.5 cm H × 2 cm W × 1.25 cm D)

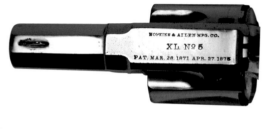

Dr. Hammond, my personal friend, met me near the house, saw the blood, touched my arm, and said with feeling: "General, your arm is broken." The last ball had passed through the elbow joint and crushed the bones into small fragments. He led me to a negro hut, large enough only for a double bed. Here I lay down, alarming an aged negro couple who feared at first that some of us might discover and seize hidden treasure which was in that bed.

Six hours later, they removed his arm.

Weapons are emblematic of power, and the fact that this gun and bullet were saved suggests that even during his lifetime, Howard's contemporaries had a sense that he would leave a historic legacy. Like several other officers from Vancouver Barracks—including Ulysses S. Grant, Philip Sheridan, George Pickett, and George C. Marshall—Howard's identity grew larger than his individual self and became a part of the American story.

Pistol
recent acquisition
(9 cm L × 3 cm W × 16 cm D)

PAINTED BRICKS & WOOD

Immediately on entering the Chief Factor's House at Fort Vancouver and taking a quick glance around the rooms, visitors can understand the authority of the Hudson's Bay Company and Dr. John McLoughlin. At this frontier post, an array of luxury goods was on display in the "Big House," including colorful dishes, silver candelabra, a gilded whale oil lamp, linens, and wool carpets. The striking backdrop to all these luxuries, however, was the brightly painted walls. Remains of the house—mainly wood and brick fragments like these—sometimes retain traces of their former colors when recovered during archaeological excavations.

Quantities of paint were imported annually to Fort Vancouver. During the spring of 1844, for example, inventories list black, blue, Spanish brown, green, white, and yellow paint. Similar colors are listed for other years, with the addition of red and Dutch Pink (which despite its name is actually a yellowish color). Usually only buildings of high social status—factors' houses and company offices at depots—were painted on the interior. The combinations were sometimes fantastical, employed to great effect on those not accustomed to colored rooms. George Ballantyne, at York Factory, noted "the painting of the room had been executed with a view to striking dumb those innocent individuals who had spent the greater part of their lives at outposts."

For visitors to the fort, McLoughlin's painted rooms would immediately have spoken of the wealth and refinement of their inhabitants. For officers and clerks working in these areas, the paint would be a symbol of their career; every time they looked up from their work, the brilliant surroundings would have reminded them of the power and reach of the Hudson's Bay Company, the enormous corporation of which they were a part.

Painted Bricks and Wood
FOVA *7837 (7.5 cm L × 7 cm W × 3 cm D), 7841 (12 cm L × 7 cm W × 5 cm D), 7843 (5 cm L × 5 cm W × 2.5 cm D), 103232 (4.5 cm L × 2 cm W × 2 cm D), 114559 (3 cm L × 2.5 cm W × 2.5 cm D), and 114577 (Largest is 4.5 cm L × 3.5 cm W × 2 cm D)*

Discharge Certificate
FOVA 120 (21.5 cm H × 31.5 cm W)

DISCHARGE CERTIFICATE, PAINTING, AMBROTYPE, & WALLET

Textual descriptions of individuals were an early technique of cementing identity, one eventually surpassed by the ability to capture an image on canvas, glass, or film. These items follow that progression, from brief words describing one's physical characteristics to painted portrait, an early type of photograph, and on to the quintessential modern identification package: the wallet.

This discharge certificate was issued to Corporal Hugh O'Byrne of the 1st Artillery in November of 1849, making it one of the earliest documents to come out of Vancouver Barracks. It is signed by Brevet-Major Hatheway, whose company had established the military post at Vancouver a mere six months before. The document tells us that O'Byrne was born in Ireland (something we might have guessed already), was five feet eight inches tall, with brown hair, blue eyes, and a fair complexion. Often these certificates even recorded scars or other distinguishing features.

This miniature painting on ivory is a rare image of Dr. David McLoughlin, John's brother, and is thought to have been done in Europe around 1838 or 1839. From using a brush to capture identity, it was a great leap to embedding a permanent and detailed likeness on glass.

Painting
recent acquisition (11.5 cm H × 8 cm W × .5 cm D)

This ambrotype, probably done in the late 1850s or early 1860s, is of John McLoughlin's three granddaughters: Margaret Rae, Maria Louisa Harvey, and Angelique Harvey.

One could argue that many people today carry their identities in their back pockets. Licenses, credit cards, receipts, photographs of loved ones—the contents of a wallet speak volumes about its owner's life. This World War II–era soldier's wallet, found under one of the Artillery Barracks porches during archaeological investigations, lacks an identifying document and money but still holds a receipt for photo developing, a calendar, and a woman's photograph. It may capture an uncommon phenomenon in archaeology: evidence of thievery, an artifact left behind by someone who was disobeying civic law as well as that imposed by military discipline.

Ambrotype
recent acquisition (9.2 cm H × 12 cm W × 1.3 cm D)

Wallet and Photograph
FOVA-3024, Lot 481 Spec 2
(8 cm H × 10 cm W × 10 cm D)

Toy Axe
FOVA 28308 (6 cm H × 3 cm W × 1.5 cm D)

Dolls
FOVA 21894 (7.5 cm H × 3.5 cm W × 2.2 cm D) and
21895 (9 cm H × 3.5 cm W × 2 cm D)

TOY AXE, DISHES, & DOLLS

Children's role-play with miniature versions of tools or household equipment helps form their adult identity. They practice parenthood, learn a trade, and gain the skills they need to survive. Childhood was short in the nineteenth century, and the children living at Vancouver would have graduated quickly from play to strenuous work and families of their own.

This toy axe was discovered at a domestic site outside the southeast corner of the Fort Vancouver stockade. Little is known about the dwelling, other than it was gone by the 1840s, when a Cooper's Shop was erected on the site. The toy is hand wrought and most likely would have been manufactured at the Blacksmith's Shop within the fort. The two dolls were recovered from the former pond in the village area, a trash dump for Vancouver Barracks. The soil layers in which they were found are believed to have been deposited between 1887 and 1894. The toy dishes are all from privies at the Quartermaster's Ranch, the residence of the military post's quartermaster and his junior officers, and so are likely playthings lost by a soldier's daughter.

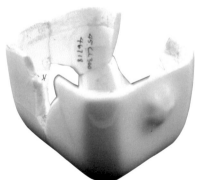

Dishes
FOVA 21672 (3 cm H × 5 cm W × 3.5 cm D)
and 21671 (3.8 cm H × 4 cm W × 2.5 cm D)

LOCKER DOOR

Graffiti reflects the common human desire to record one's identity in association with a specific place. It might be on "home turf," or it might reflect a foray into someone else's territory. It sometimes marks brave progress along a travel route, as when American immigrants recorded their names alongside the Oregon Trail. It might be an effort to record one's identity in the shadow of loss, as for Lady Jane Grey when she (or one of her supporters) carved the Latin version of her name, "IANE," on a wall in the Tower of London while awaiting execution.

An exceptional artifact from a barracks building that was demolished in the 1950s captures a brief moment in time, when Italian prisoners-of-war were incarcerated here during World War II. This wooden locker door has a signed inscription, written in pencil by one of the POWS. These men had a unique place in Vancouver society. Though they were kept in the guardhouse at first, they later bunked in regular barracks and frequently left the post for picnics, religious services, and visits to the cinema. The message reads:

A
P.O.W.
WHO ^{HAS} ~~WAS~~ BEEN IN THIS
PLEACE FOR A [ILLEGIBLE] TO DAY
3 FEB 1946, LEAVE TO ITALY
FULL OF HAPPYNESS
THANK YOU FOR EVERYTHING
YOU PEOPLE DID FOR US
GOOD BYE FOR NOW
AND GOOD LUCK TO YOU
THIS IS FOR THE SOLDIER WHO TAKE MY
BED PLEACE

Locker Door
recent acquisition
(220 cm H × 50 cm W
× 1.5 cm D)

Pipe
FOVA 3734 (5 cm H × 2.5 cm W × 3 cm D)

PIPES

Frequently, an artifact reflects the cultural identity of a group through traditional artistic styles. Less often, it can reveal the merging of these styles, a tangible product of cultural exchange. These pipes may be two examples of such a phenomenon. The raven pipe—found within the fort near the southeast corner—is Haida in form, yet may incorporate design elements traditionally employed by Coast Salish tribes. The other pipe is an anthropomorphic shape, a human male with a flattened head suggesting Chinookan people of the Lower Columbia River. The archaeologist who excavated this piece noted, however, that there are designs on the cheeks that resemble Hawaiian facial tattooing. This pipe was found at the site of House 2, a dwelling on the east side of the Fort Vancouver Village.

Pipe
FOVA 11212 (4.5 cm H × 4 cm W × 1.5 cm D)

TRANSFERPRINTED CERAMICS, COTTAGEWARE SLOP BOWL, & POLYCHROME PLATE (CONTINUED ON NEXT PAGE)

When everyone at Fort Vancouver shopped at the same store and chose from among the same limited array of goods, how can consumer choice reflect individual identity? Even faced with such restrictions, the employees and their families made their material possessions reflect individual preferences or cultural backgrounds.

The analysis of ceramics throughout the site shows that households, both inside the fort and within the village, had many of the same types. Trends in color and pattern choice, as well as vessel type, may provide clues to identity. Some of that variety is shown here. The transfer-printed plates (all patterns manufactured by

Transferprinted Ceramics
FOVA 36074 (4 cm H × 25 cm DIAM.), 1739 (2.5 cm H × 22.5 cm DIAM.),
36389 (15 cm H × 18 cm W × 3 cm D), 319 (7.62 cm H × 12.7 cm DIAM.)
and 7089 (16.5 cm L × 13.5 cm W × 2 cm D)

Cottageware Slop Bowl
FOVA 652 (7.5 CM H × 14.5 CM DIAM.)

the Spode Company of England: blue British Flowers, green Seasons, black Chinese Plants, and brown Continental Views) and teacup (pink French Radiating Sprigs) were all recovered from the fort site, as was the hand-painted cottageware slop bowl. The multicolored plate with a bird design is the MacCartney pattern made by John Ridgway between 1830 and 1855, a red transferprinted base design overlaid by hand painting and gilding. Many serving pieces in this pattern were found at the site of the industrial complex near the village pond; the fact that they have not been found elsewhere at Fort Vancouver, or indeed at any Hudson's Bay Company site, suggests that the set was not purchased at the Company Sale Shop but was an heirloom or a special personal order.

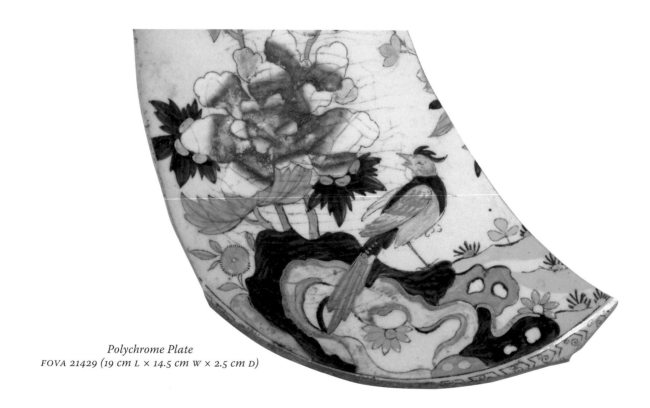

Polychrome Plate
FOVA 21429 (19 CM L × 14.5 CM W × 2.5 CM D)

JEWELRY CLASP & BUTTONS

In 1841, Lieutenant Charles Wilkes described Fort Vancouver's village as "fifty comfortable houses…swarming with children, whites, half-breeds, and pure Indians." In 1854, Isaac Ebey wrote that the village houses were "old, dilapidated huts." Documented by the artifacts that remain, juxtaposed next to the biased accounts of observers, lies the story of the village. This jeweled clasp and these blue Prosser-type buttons were found in Fort Vancouver's village, at a dwelling known today simply as House 2. Without detailed and unbiased historical records describing its inhabitants, interpreting the structure to visitors can be challenging. Who lived within its walls? How can the interior be recreated to most accurately reflect the original décor? Faced with the most basic of questions regarding domestic arrangements, we turn to the archaeological remains. Since objects like these are usually worn by a woman, the presence of these artifacts suggests that a family lived in House 2 rather than bachelors bunking together.

Jewelry Clasp
FOVA 37150 (8.80 mm H × 10.94 mm W × 8.30 mm D)

Buttons
FOVA 3650 (3.06 mm H × 10.54 mm DIAM. each)

TECHNOLOGY

From Stone Tools to Modern Technology

◈ *Robert J. Cromwell*

WHEN PEOPLE SPEAK about technology, they often think of the gadgets and tools we rely on in our everyday world: computers, the Internet, cellular "smart" telephones, and iPods, for example. These are the artifacts of our modern age, merely the latest developments that help define our society. Every culture through time has had its own technological breakthroughs, its own material objects that were developed and manipulated to help individuals survive and thrive in their specific environments.

One of the technologies in almost every area of the world where humans have lived is the manipulation of stone into tools. Our earliest ancestors left evidence of their lives in the Olduvai Gorge of Africa in simple large chopping stones that date to over 2.5 million years ago. Stone tools, or lithic technology, gave way to highly developed projectile point forms, sharpened tips, and blades that could be affixed to spears, arrows and in some cultures, to swords. As recently as two hundred years ago, the indigenous people who resided along the banks of the Columbia were making highly refined arrowheads that were often sharper than surgical steel.

This is one example of how our modern mindset regarding technology may obscure our perceptions of another group's artifacts. We may see stone tools as primitive compared to our phones and computers, but they were highly developed implements requiring specialized skills to create. The ability to use and maintain tools allowed people to survive in some of the harshest environments in the world or, in the case of the Pacific Northwest, to live in relatively high population densities.

The technology represented in the collection at Fort Vancouver links our modern industrial and information age with the ages that preceded it. Within the collection are objects that would have been familiar to ancient Romans (such as hand-wrought nails and door pintles) as well as objects of unusual modernity that are recognizable to almost every visitor who enters the park today (such as ceramic tablewares, toothbrushes, and silverware). People living in the nineteenth century saw incredible strides in the fields of science, medicine, engineering, and industrial design and production, and these advances are displayed in the park's collection of objects.

The Hudson's Bay Company, as a British Royal Charter corporation, made it a policy to supply its posts with material goods predominantly manufactured in England. Between 1825 and 1844, annual shipments of nearly 200 tons of goods were transported over 17,000 miles by ships sailing directly from London. At the time, London was arguably the most industrialized city in the world, and Vancouver was at the farthest reaches of the British Empire. Due to the Hudson's Bay Company, this remote land, separated from London by a six-month ocean voyage, became the emporium of industrial goods and technology on the west coast of what would become the United States.

The employees of the Company were paid in credit, to be spent only in the Company stores. It is of little surprise, therefore, that the archaeological assemblages from the households of the richest and poorest residents of the fort are remarkably similar. Both display the breadth of British manufactured industrial goods imported to the site. During the heyday of the fort, the Company's Sale Shop and Indian Trade Shop were the only stores in town, and some of the newest goods that England had to offer were on sale within their walls.

Fort Vancouver was the location of many technological firsts in the Pacific Northwest. Although the first use of iron plows for agriculture on the coast north of Spanish California is documented at Fort Astoria in 1811, farm operations around Fort Vancouver during the late

1820s provided the Pacific Northwest's first cultivated wheat, apples, and peaches, now considered regional crops. The farm at Fort Astoria (later renamed Fort George) never exceeded 80 acres, whereas over 1,200 acres were farmed around Fort Vancouver by the mid 1830s, necessitating the first widespread use of horse-drawn plows. The first mechanical, water-powered sawmill and gristmill in the Pacific Northwest were at Fort Vancouver by about 1828. The mill sites were three miles upstream from the fort, on the north bank of the Columbia River (near where I-205 crosses the river today). The use of steam-powered propulsion in the Pacific Northwest was initiated with the arrival of the Hudson's Bay Company trading ship *Beaver* in 1836.

Another driving force of technological development in the past two hundred years has been the military. As global politics impacted the Hudson's Bay Company and this location formally became United States territory in 1846, the influence of British culture on the area waned. The U.S. Army arrived at Fort Vancouver in May of 1849 with a detachment of the U.S. First Artillery aboard the U.S.S. *Massachusetts*. The Army brought an assortment of objects and weaponry that was technologically comparable to that employed by the Hudson's Bay Company, but all of this would change within the next two decades.

With the close of the American Civil War in 1865, Vancouver Barracks saw an immediate influx of American soldiers who brought new weaponry of war. The smoothbore muskets and paper cartridges of the pre-1860s Army were replaced by rifled muskets and rifles, and muzzle-loading weaponry was replaced by breech-loaded weapons with self-contained metallic cartridges. The Army established the Vancouver Arsenal in about 1856, and thousands of military rounds were manufactured there for use in campaigns throughout the West until 1884.

Warfare became an ever-mechanized affair by the dawn of the twentieth century, and a striking display of the transition of the horse-mobile Army to the machine-mobile Army is evident in the experiments with fixed-wing aircraft on the post's polo fields in 1909, a precursor to the later Pearson Field.

With the United States' entry into World War I, the Army responded to the industrial necessity for natural resources extraction.

While labor disputes were crippling the Pacific Northwest's lumber industry, the Allied forces in Europe were demanding spruce wood for the newest technological weapon, the airplane. Nearly 30,000 American Doughboys served their country in 1917 and 1918, not wielding rifles in the trenches of France but wielding axes and controlling steam-powered equipment in the woods of the Pacific Northwest as part of the Army's Spruce Production Division. The nationalization of the lumber industry had long-lasting effects. The mill and the logging camps were primarily serviced by railroads, but for the first time, the Army brought widespread use of trucks into the logging industry, a practice that continues to this day.

The American society of the early twenty-first century associates technology with the computer- and internet-based gadgets and tools that so many people use every day. We are accustomed to the rapid pace of development, or "Moore's Law," which states that the speed of computer processors will roughly double every two years. A five-year-old computer or cell phone is usually considered old technology. As a result, it is becoming more difficult to see the many technological links between the past, the present, and the future. The artifact collection at Fort Vancouver reminds us of these connections, of the varied technologies that allowed people to live in the Columbia River Basin for thousands of years, to colonize the area for a European corporation, and finally to settle and develop the area as we know it today.

STONE PROJECTILE POINTS, GROUND STONE, & METAL PROJECTILE POINT

One of the longest surviving technologies across the globe is the use of stones as tools. The collection at Fort Vancouver has hundreds of chert and obsidian projectile points such as these, as well as ground stone tools, like this mortar and pestle, and these manos. Meriwether Lewis, on the subject of the people of the Lower Columbia, wrote: "the bow and arrow is the most common instrument among them, every man being furnished with them whether he has a gun or not; this instrument is imployed [*sic*] indiscriminately in hunting every species of animal on which they subsist."

The sparse scatter of points across most of the Fort Vancouver site is likely related to periodic hunting activities. Certain areas, poorly known as of yet, appear to be more developed, perhaps representing seasonal fishing camps or villages. Continuing the tradition, certain inhabitants of the village seem to have used shaped-stone tools to augment their more Western tool kits. Iron projectile points represent a blending of technologies. The Company blacksmiths are known to have made these points for trade with the local Indians.

Stone Projectile Points
FOVA 21830 (4 cm L × 3 cm W × .5 cm D),
21831 (3.5 cm L × 1 cm W × .3 cm D), and
21834 (4 cm L × 2 cm W × .5 cm D)

Ground Stone Manos
FOVA 2306 (17.5 cm H × 6.5 cm W × 4 cm D) and
2305 (9 cm H × 7 cm W × 4.5 cm D)

Mortar & Pestle
FOVA 2312 (15 cm H × 23 cm. DIAM.) and
2311 (17.5 cm H × 9.5 cm DIAM at base, 5 cm DIAM at top)

Metal Projectile Point
FOVA 125364 (6.7 cm L × 2.3 cm W)

BEAVER TRAP

Perhaps the best representation of the purpose of the Hudson's Bay Company is the iron beaver trap. Traps such as these were used by Company employees on their yearly fur brigades into the interior of the Northwest to harvest beaver pelts for the hat-making industry in England. Like the woodsman's axe or the miner's pick and shovel, the beaver trap was an iconic tool, crucial for the extraction of pelts for European and Asian markets. It symbolizes the vast wealth of raw materials that could be taken from what newcomers saw as the frontier. The beaver trap also symbolizes the introduction of changes to the environment that humans initiated during the colonial period.

To protect the regions of abundant beaver to the north of Fort Vancouver, the Hudson's Bay Company intentionally destroyed or "trapped out" the reserves of beaver in the Snake River Country to the east. The beaver trap was the means of accomplishing this eradication. They created a "fur desert" by over-trapping, thereby preventing Americans from encroaching on the British company's territory. As Jennifer Ott posits, this practice may have had dramatic effects on the Columbia River watershed, including impacts to soil, water, vegetation, and other animal species.

Individual fragments of traps have been recovered at Fort Vancouver, but to date, no intact examples have been found. The photo shows a recreated beaver trap, manufactured by the blacksmiths at Fort Vancouver National Historic Site, and a partially reconstructed trap from archaeological deposits. Historically, traps were manufactured on site by Hudson's Bay Company blacksmiths.

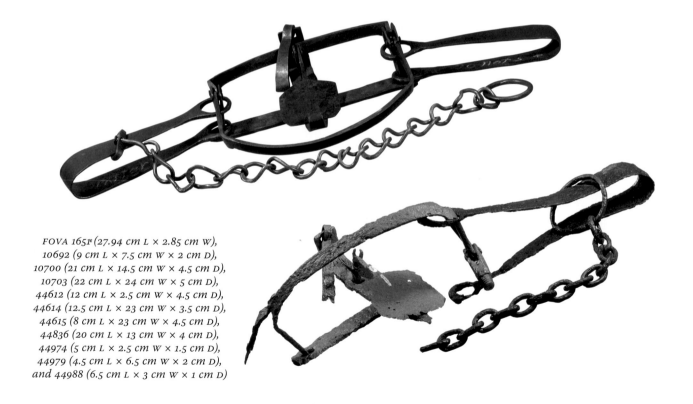

FOVA 1651ʳ (27.94 cm L × 2.85 cm W),
10692 (9 cm L × 7.5 cm W × 2 cm D),
10700 (21 cm L × 14.5 cm W × 4.5 cm D),
10703 (22 cm L × 24 cm W × 5 cm D),
44612 (12 cm L × 2.5 cm W × 4.5 cm D),
44614 (12.5 cm L × 23 cm W × 3.5 cm D),
44615 (8 cm L × 23 cm W × 4.5 cm D),
44836 (20 cm L × 13 cm W × 4 cm D),
44974 (5 cm L × 2.5 cm W × 1.5 cm D),
44979 (4.5 cm L × 6.5 cm W × 2 cm D),
and 44988 (6.5 cm L × 3 cm W × 1 cm D)

TRADE AXES

The axe was an essential piece of technology for the trappers and Indians of the Pacific Northwest. Lieutenant Charles Wilkes, an American naval officer and head of the United States Exploring Expedition, visited Fort Vancouver in 1841. He suggested that "a trapper's success, in fact, depends on his axe; and on this being lost or broken, he necessarily relinquishes his labors, and returns unsuccessful. I was surprised at seeing the celerity with which these axes are made. Fifty of them, it is said, can be manufactured in a day, and twenty-five are accounted an ordinary day's work. They are eagerly sought after by the Indians, who are very particular that the axe should have a certain shape, somewhat like a tomahawk."

Part of the utility of large artifact collections is the ability to display attributes of technology, such as manufacturing techniques and the evolution of styles through time. The two axe heads on the left are typical Hudson's Bay Company trade axes. The one on the far left was only partially manufactured, showing how Company blacksmiths would manufacture an axe head from one piece of wrought iron, wrapped back on itself. The blade area of the axe would then be welded together. The finished axe head in the middle demonstrates how these techniques can be difficult to ascertain from finished pieces.

The Hudson's Bay Company trade axe has antecedents in French technologies of the Middle Ages that can also be traced to Celtic technology of the Roman Empire period. They were probably manufactured in the thousands at Fort Vancouver to exchange with Indians for pelts. Some of the axes recovered from Fort Vancouver are marked with an "AM"; these may be the maker's mark of Alan Morrison, who was a blacksmith at the post between at least 1838 and 1841. The axe head on the far right is a mid nineteenth-century "American" style, with a broader blade and a flattened poll that could also be used as a hammer.

FOVA 30668 (16 cm L × 5 cm W × 4 cm D), 197398 (18 cm L × 9.5 cm W × 4.5 cm D), and 2232 (19 cm L × 12.5 cm W × 3 cm D)

PLOW SHARE & SICKLE BLADE

T. J. Farnham described the Fort Vancouver agricultural enterprises around 1843 in these words: "And behold the Vancouver farm, stretching up and down the river—3,000 acres, fenced into beautiful fields—sprinkled with dairy houses, and herd men and shepherd's cottages! A busy place is this." The large-scale agriculture surrounding Fort Vancouver depended on a sizable workforce. Livestock-drawn plows alleviated the burden somewhat, enabling large tracts of land to be tilled relatively quickly. This plow share, found within the fort proper, was possibly being stored or repaired.

To a large extent, harvesting was still done by hand, though John McLoughlin did order a horse-powered thresher in 1836. This sickle, identical to those that would have been used to cut grains in the fields around the fort, was found at the site of the Sale Shop, suggesting that it was an item marketed to American settlers or missionaries. Farnham, while writing glowingly of the Hudson's Bay Company's "immense farm" and other improvements, was unapologetically pro-American, accusing the British fur-trading company of economic retaliation against Willamette Valley settlers. He accused the Company of withholding access to retail goods for settlers who attempted to trade with the Indians for furs.

Plow Share
FOVA 394 (38 cm L × 18 cm W × 21 cm D)

Sickle Blade
FOVA 750 (38.5 cm L × 12 cm W × 1 cm D)

BOILER PLATE & BRACKET

This fragment of riveted boiler plate and bracket were recovered from a former pond near the fort. The first steam-powered ship in the Pacific Northwest was the Hudson's Bay Company's *Beaver*, which arrived at Fort Vancouver on April 10, 1836. The *Beaver* was designed to convert from sail to steam power depending on sea conditions. On its initial voyage from England, it was outfitted solely for sailing. The ship's engines and boilers had been dismantled and stowed. They were re-assembled at Fort Vancouver at the boat sheds near the Columbia River, indicating that Company employees were familiar with steam boilers at this time. The *Beaver* left Fort Vancouver on June 18, 1836, never to return, as it was used as a trade and research vessel around Vancouver Island and along the Canadian coast for the next thirty years. The ship was wrecked on the rocks of Prospect Point, at the entrance to Vancouver Harbor, in 1888. It is interesting to speculate about the origins of these boiler plate fragments, as the shipyards were adjacent to the pond. Their presence indicates that the Hudson's Bay Company had dealings with steam technology prior to abandoning the site in 1860.

Boiler Plate
FOVA 94473 (13.5 CM H × 18 CM W × 3 CM D) and
100363 (5 CM H × 15 CM W × 5 CM D)

Bracket
FOVA 100363 (5 CM H × 15 CM W × 5 CM D)

Wound Bead
FOVA 7981 (10.54 mm H
× 10.34 mm DIAM.)

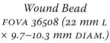

Wound Bead
FOVA 36508 (22 mm L
× 9.7–10.3 mm DIAM.)

Wound Bead
FOVA 36512
(11.1–12.4 mm L
× 12.3–13.4 mm DIAM.)

Wound Beads
FOVA 29978 (7–9.3 mm L
× 8–10 mm DIAM.)

BEADS

Beads were the currency of the fur trade, and the Hudson's Bay Company imported literally thousands of pounds of European and Chinese glass trade beads to Fort Vancouver each year between 1825 and 1850. The importance of beads to Northwest Indians was established early in the fur trade period. Lewis and Clark wrote of the preference for blue beads among the people of the Columbia River. Regarding the Clatsop who lived at the mouth of the river, Lewis wrote: "these coarse blue beads are their f[av]orite merchandize, and are called by them *tia Commáshuck* or Chiefs beads. The best wampum is not so much esteemed by them as the most inferior beads." McLoughlin noted the insistence of the Indian traders on high-quality goods: "the Aqua Marina coliers [strands of beads] do not suit the fancy of the natives," he wrote to the Governor and Committee of the Hudson's Bay Company on July 6, 1827: "the Bead sent as Sample to England (and as a Substitute for which these Coliers have been sent) was imported from China…"

In the archaeological collection at Fort Vancouver, there are over 150,000 beads that have been recovered from the site. Lester Ross's 1990 archaeological analysis of over 104,000 of them documented over 150 varieties. Although diminutive in size, beads came in a multitude of colors and shapes and were created with a range of manufacturing techniques. Those techniques leave definable attributes that allow specific bead types to be dated within specific decades of manufacture.

Wound Beads. These beads demonstrate the oldest manufacturing technique for glass beads: wound, or "lamp wound," manufacturing. They show the intricacy or simplicity of decoration available on beads of the early fur trade period in the Pacific Northwest. Lamp-wound beads were manufactured one at a time, utilizing an open-flamed lamp that would heat glass wands until they were molten. The softened wand would then be wound around a piece of wire. This enabled a bead manu-facturer to apply polychrome decorations in unique patterns or leave just a single color. The undecorated blue wound beads appear to represent the "Chief's," "China," or "Canton" beads of the fur trade of the Pacific Northwest. The faceted beads (FOVA 29978, previous page) were decorated further through the use of a grinding wheel. Individual facets would be ground into the surface of the bead after it had cooled and hardened.

Drawn Beads. The most common manufac-turing technique for beads of the nineteenth century was the "drawn" and "hot tumbled" style. Drawn beads were manufactured with a hollow tube of glass, which was heated until molten, then pulled in opposite directions, stretching the glass lengthwise while shrink-ing its diameter. The tube would then be cut into thousands of individual segments and tumbled in a hot pan to remove the sharpened edges. The simplest form of manufacturing glass beads is termed the "cane" bead. These were created by simply cutting or snapping hollow glass canes into various segments. This example (FOVA 36606) was been hot tumbled in a pan to remove the sharpened burrs. FOVA 36915 demonstrates how many individual wands of multi-colored glass could be combined, heated, and stretched together into one strand of beads. FOVA 52486 shows the multiple sizes that could result from this manufacturing technique. Just like the wound beads, drawn beads were often decorated with individual facets created with a grinding wheel, as seen on FOVA 36575. Interestingly, Ross noted that white drawn beads were much more prevalent than those of any other color at Fort Vancouver.

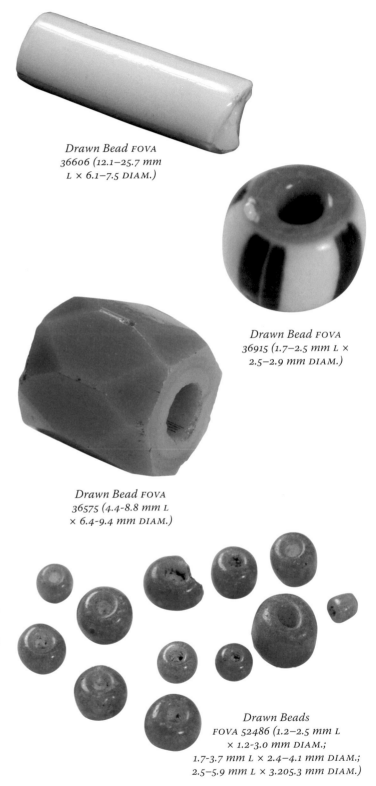

Drawn Bead FOVA 36606 (12.1–25.7 mm L × 6.1–7.5 DIAM.)

Drawn Bead FOVA 36915 (1.7–2.5 mm L × 2.5–2.9 mm DIAM.)

Drawn Bead FOVA 36575 (4.4-8.8 mm L × 6.4-9.4 mm DIAM.)

Drawn Beads FOVA 52486 (1.2–2.5 mm L × 1.2-3.0 mm DIAM.; 1.7-3.7 mm L × 2.4–4.1 mm DIAM.; 2.5–5.9 mm L × 3.205.3 mm DIAM.)

Wrought Nails
FOVA 186030 (7 cm L × .5 cm W × .5 cm D)

WROUGHT NAILS, CUT NAILS, & WIRE NAILS

One of the most recognizable artifacts in the collection at Fort Vancouver is the iron nail. The hand-wrought nails used by the Hudson's Bay Company from the 1820s to the 1840s would have been recognizable to blacksmiths in the time of the Roman Empire. Machine-cut nails represent a major technological shift. Developed in the 1820s and common by the 1850s, machine-cut nails allowed a blacksmith to almost triple the production rate. The common wire-drawn nail we are familiar with today—faster and cheaper to manufacture—was also first developed in the 1820s but only became common in the United States after the 1860s and, here in the Pacific Northwest, is generally dated to after 1900. These nails originate from the 2004 excavations of the fort's Powder Magazine and the southern edge of the warehouse known as the New Store. The hand-wrought nails represent the construction of these buildings in about 1830. The cut nails represent American imports used by the Hudson's Bay Company to maintain the buildings, probably in about 1845. The wire nails are from loading docks and other facilities of the U.S. Army's spruce mill, which covered the area during World War I.

Cut Nails
FOVA 185742, 185748, 185717, 185659, 185674, and 185686
(3.79 cm L–7.7 cm L)

Wire Nails
FOVA 185873 (8.94 cm L)

MUSKET BALLS, GUNFLINTS, MINIÉ BALLS, DRAGON SIDE PLATE, CANNON PRIMER, & CARTRIDGES
(CONTINUED ON NEXT PAGE)

Almost the entire history of the development of black-powder weapons from the nineteenth century to World War II is represented in the Fort Vancouver archaeological collection. The Hudson's Bay Company provided its employees and trading partners with flintlock muskets that fired round lead musket balls. These weapons would have been familiar to soldiers who fought in the American Revolutionary War, as well as to members of the Lewis & Clark Expedition. The significance of these weapons is demonstrated by the amount of black powder, stored in the fort's Powder Magazine, that was necessary for firing them. The spring 1844 inventory lists over 14,000 pounds of powder in 1,586 barrels and kegs.

The musket balls and gunflints shown here were all recovered from the fort's Sale Shop and were imported from England for trade to Company employees and American settlers. There were at least two sizes of musket balls, plus buckshot, beavershot, and birdshot in at least five size grades. The gunflints are found in four sizes, probably corresponding to pistol and musket sizes. The dragon side plate is from the quintessential fur trade musket known as the "Northwest Gun."

The U.S. Army arrived in 1849, and by the late 1850s, it was issuing "Minié" balls, which were conically formed to allow for better trajectory. These projectiles were the most commonly used bullets during the American Civil War. In late October or early November 1858, the ordinance depot at Fort Vancouver, operated by Lieutenant Joshua Sill, had on hand 8,000 musket rifled ball cartridges, 9,000 Harper's Ferry rifled ball cartridges, 142,000 Sharps carbine ball cartridges, 39,000 Colts belt pistol cartridges, and 27,000 Colts dragoon pistol ball cartridges. All of these would have included formed paper cartridges. The

Musket Balls
FOVA 2996 *(.5 CM DIAM.)*

Gunflints
FOVA 79189 *(Largest is 3 cm L × 2 cm W × 1 cm D)*

Minié Ball
FOVA 196579 *(1.5 CM DIAM.)*

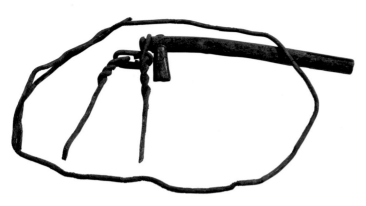

Cannon Primer
FOVA 2013 *(9.5 cm L × 5 cm W × .5 cm D)*

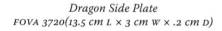

Dragon Side Plate
FOVA 3720 *(13.5 cm L × 3 cm W × .2 cm D)*

Minié ball shown here was recovered from the area of the Vancouver Arsenal and represents some of the hundreds of thousands of munitions manufactured and stored there in the mid nineteenth century.

By the late 1860s, the U.S. Army had switched to breech-loading weaponry with metallic cartridge cases, including the .45-70 cartridge common in the Indian Wars of the 1870s and the .30-06 Springfield round, which was the standard caliber of the U.S. Army during World Wars I and II. The Vancouver Arsenal at Fort Vancouver manufactured and supplied Springfield cartridges for the 1872 Modoc War, General O. O. Howard's 1877 campaign against the Nez Perce, and the 1878 Bannock and Paiute War. The .45-70 cartridges were recovered from within the Fort Vancouver stockade and represent a skirmish training field there after the Hudson's Bay Company's departure. The stamp on the end of the cartridge indicates it was made for the Springfield trapdoor rifle at the Frankfurt Arsenal in January 1884.

Cartridges
FOVA 52388 *(6.5 cm L × 1.2 cm DIAM.)*

HORSESHOE, MULESHOE, TRUCK PLATE, RAILROAD CAR BRAKE SHOE HOLDER, & RAILROAD SPIKE
(CONTINUED ON NEXT PAGE)

Transportation changed rapidly from the mid nineteenth to the mid twentieth century. The use of horses for transportation goes back thousands of years in the Old World, and horses were adopted by indigenous groups in parts of the Americas during the Spanish colonial period. Horses were introduced into the Lower Columbia River Basin, however, by the Hudson's Bay Company in the 1820s. Patricia Erigero suggests: "Horses were probably the most important and practical animals at the fort, necessary for all overland travel, both as mounts and as pack animals and, occasionally, as food, and for work on the farm." The U.S. Army also depended on horses and mules. In May 1849, the U.S. Army sent the Regiment of Mounted Riflemen to the Oregon Territory with 700 horses, 1200 mules, oxen, and 171 wagons. This was the first military march across the length of the Oregon Trail. Major Osborne Cross, quartermaster for the regiment, wrote: "The plains which we passed over for days and weeks through dust and heat, and sometimes thirst, are enough to appal [sic] the stoutest hearts..." After the ordeal of the trip, he described Fort Vancouver: "This place would be a fine location for troops, and indeed is the only spot between here and the mouth of the river where the mountains will admit of it." Horses and mules continued to be used by the U.S. Army into the 1940s. The Army also used horses for recreation, playing polo in matches between officers during the 1920s and 1930s.

In 1853, prior to serving as major general in the Civil War and running for president, Captain George B. McClellan explored (via horse and mule) a route for the Pacific railroad from Fort Vancouver on the Klickitat trail across the Cascade Mountains to the west. While the development of the intercontinental railroad system revolutionized the overland transportation system in the 1860s, the intercontinental railroad envisioned by the McClellan survey did not come to the

Muleshoe
FOVA 30713 (2.5 cm H × 9 cm W × 14 cm D)

Horseshoe
FOVA 30695 (3 cm H × 13 cm W × 16 cm D)

*Railroad Car Brake
Shoe Holder*
FOVA 11186 (12 cm H ×
35 cm W × 8 cm D)

Truck Plate
FOVA-3047 Lot 252 Spec 1
(7.5 cm H × 10 cm × .2 cm D)

Railroad Spike
FOVA 52375 (14 cm L × 3.5 cm W × 4.5 cm D)

Pacific Northwest until 1883 and did not enter Vancouver until about 1906. Its arrival is represented in the railroad spike found within the area of the former fort stockade. The Pacific Northwest's largest contribution to World War I was the extraction and production of lumber. The U.S. Army nationalized the lumber industry in 1917, constructing the world's largest lumber mill at the time on the sites of Fort Vancouver and Pearson Field. Raw lumber was imported on rail spurs, and the finished product was hauled out to the main line and directed east to manufacturing plants.

The nature of the transition from the historic fur trade post to an industrial mill site was noted in the monthly bulletin of the Spruce Production Division: "The old days of Vancouver Post have gone; the new days are here. Time has transformed the former Indian trading grounds into a huge war site where scores of steel and wooden ships are building, any one of which would carry a whole fleet of the 'great ships' of the early days; where thirty thousand khaki soldiers now have their headquarters; where wild animals no longer roam the forests that once teemed with bear and deer, and all manner of furry game; where the Government's huge sawmill devours whole forests in a single day, its saws shrieking through the thousand-year-old logs with a sinister shrillness that puts the ancient tribal warwhoop to a whispering shame! Yet it's all the same place." The spruce mill also saw the first large-scale use of automobiles and trucks in the lumber industry. The truck plate was found during the 2005 excavations of the Hudson's Bay Company garden. Excavation of a hardened dirt road surface from World War I yielded the truck plate, along with metal fasteners for canvas truck canopies.

AIRCRAFT FABRIC

This circular patch of doped aircraft fabric was recovered from underneath the circa-1904 U.S. Army munitions structure at Pearson Air Field. This type of fabric is consistent with aircraft fabric of the early twentieth century and likely denotes aircraft maintenance activities done by the U.S. Army Air Corps units based at Pearson between about 1923 and 1941. It may have been cut from one of the 321st Curtiss JN-4 "Jennies" or similar aircraft. It appears that the swatch was cut from the aircraft using a drill, perforating a basic circle that was then punched out to allow access to an interior portion of an airplane. One of the more epic flights of these interwar-era planes was made by Lieutenant Oakley Kelly, head of the 321st Observation Squadron at Pearson Field. One year after his pioneering non-stop transcontinental flight in April 1923, he took Oregon Trail veteran Ezra Meeker on a flight from Vancouver Barracks to air races at Dayton, Ohio. Meeker, who founded the Oregon Trail Foundation, had taken six months to travel to Oregon from the Midwest by ox team in 1852. The flight by open cockpit airplane lasted a single day of flying time.

Aircraft Fabric
FOVA 160125 (5.5 CM DIAM.)

GLOBALIZATION

New Iterations of Old Patterns of Change

◈ *Heidi K. Pierson*

IN OUR MODERN WORLD of transnational corporations and debates about whether global markets improve or detract from our lives and those of people in developing countries, it is hard to see history and archaeology's relevance. How does a modern tennis shoe—manufactured in China, India, or Brazil and marketed across the United States, Canada, and Western Europe—compare with a piece of pottery, a clay pipe, or an ornate button found at Fort Vancouver? The rate and pace of modern change seem so rapid and immediate that discussions of the fate of nations, world economies, and global connectedness seem far removed from the architecture, clothing, and speech of history. Nevertheless, globalization, related to the movement of people, products, industrial production, and ideas, has a long history. Our understanding of migration patterns, the effects of new products, and the modern world market cannot be understood without reference to the past two hundred years of change.

Of course, people were moving around the world long before written history. In the historic period, companies like the Hudson's Bay Company and the British East India Company expanded deep into contested territories, their motive being trade and the great profits that could be made from natural resources. There are many ways to define globalization, but here we look at it in terms of the past. The following characterization by Giddens is apt for our purposes: globalization is the increase of social relationships worldwide; these relationships link distant places in such a way that activities in each place are shaped by events occurring elsewhere.

From the fifteenth to the nineteenth century, the interaction between local and regional settlements and their far-flung administrative centers was part of the story of globalization. In the case of Fort Vancouver, the fort itself was the regional headquarters of a company administered from England—17,000 nautical miles away. At Fort Vancouver, we have uncovered objects from around the world. Stoneware jars from England and China; decorative tablewares from England, France, China, and Japan; English brick; Hawaiian coral (used to make mortar); even buttons made in England for a Haitian King. There are many ways to consider these objects. Some artifacts represent early capitalism and the imposition—both overt and unintentional—of colonial values. Others represent the spread of indigenous plants and traditions from the New World to the Old early in the colonization of the Americas.

Fort Vancouver was a hub of activity, a place where people from Hawaii, Portugal, Scotland, and England mingled with Métis and French-Canadians and with Indians from diverse tribes. Often the men employed by the Company were married to local women, a tradition that had persisted since the early days of the fur trade. Consider walking through this crowd, the ways people might be dressed, the things they would be carrying, and so on. Consider that most of the trade goods available in the area were from the Hudson's Bay Company stores. The people of the fort distinguished themselves from each other through their use of what are now artifacts in addition to the types of objects they possessed. The impact of this input of global products and ideas was tremendous, on both the way of life of indigenous people and those from faraway places.

The arrival of missionaries Marcus and Narcissa Whitman heralded an influx of Americans to the Pacific Northwest, bedraggled survivors of the Oregon Trail who were often near starving and running out of supplies. Though the land claim question (the American or British ownership of the region) had yet to be settled and the Company could not stop immigrants from coming, the Hudson's Bay Company officially discouraged any aid to these immigrants. John McLoughlin's assistance to the settlers was controversial. The tensions between nations over an area that had been dominated by a transnational company were played out in a colonial drama that was directed by the region's natural resources, its remoteness, and the technology and cultures of the nineteenth century.

As Americans took over the area, they first traded with the Hudson's Bay Company, but eventually bought goods from an array of trading partners. During the U.S. Army period, Japanese pottery became common as the Japanese market was opened to the West. Ceramics in general came from a diversifying range of sources—many representing new American-made wares.

After the Hudson's Bay Company moved to British Columbia, Fort Vancouver began to reflect a tendency toward U.S. trade protectionism that was ascendant at the time. Artifacts of U.S. manufacture are more prevalent in late nineteenth and early twentieth century contexts, illustrating the tendency for global trade regimes to wax and wane as individual nations decide to limit international trade in order to give a boost to their own (often fledgling) industries. Whether the present form of globalization is a new phenomena or merely represents the newest iteration of an old pattern remains to be seen. Aspects of the processes of the global shift of the world economy, reflected in modern conceptions of globalization, are also seen in many of the historical objects recovered from Fort Vancouver.

Clay Tobacco Pipe
FOVA 15003 (4.5 CM H × 2.25 CM W)

TOBACCO PIPES

Tobacco pipes are interesting because they represent two distinct threads of culture associated with the smoking of tobacco. Pipes made in England and Scotland litter the site. These white clay pipes were cheap and disposable, and according to many contemporary writers, smoking was very popular here. Dunn, for example, wrote of Fort Vancouver: "The voyageur and the trapper, who have traversed thousands of miles through wild and unfrequented regions; and the mariner, who has circumnavigated the globe, may be found grouped together, smoking, joking, singing, and story telling; and in every way banishing *dull care* till the period of their again setting out for their respective destinations arrive." We also have carved stone pipes; this pipe is of Indian origin. While this pipe is also for smoking tobacco, it is probable that it was used quite differently than the imported clay pipes. Dunn commented on the smoking habits of the Indians of the lower Columbia, indicating that "smoking rites precede every matter of great importance; and sometimes they are politic." The carved stone pipes found at Fort Vancouver were probably not disposable in the same way as the clay pipes, and may have been associated with ceremonial uses rather than casual tobacco smoking.

Stone Tobacco Pipe
FOVA 694 (3.5 CM H × 5 CM W × 1.5 CM D)

Clay Tobacco Pipe
FOVA 2009 (14 CM L × .5 CM DIAM (stem),
10 CM L × 3.5 CM DIAM. (bowl section)

BRITISH WILLOW PLATE
& CHINESE "WILLOW" PLATE

This popular blue and white pattern (bottom) is often mistaken for a Chinese-produced item like this top example. In fact, it was produced in Staffordshire, England. The Staffordshire potteries used transferprinted patterns on relatively cheap earthenwares to produce affordable copies of previously unaffordable luxuries. The sale of such products in the Pacific Northwest during the mid 1800s represents the movement of a design aesthetic from China through Europe and into the American frontier.

Chinese "Willow" Plate
FOVA 317 *(3 cm H × 22.5 cm W × 18.5 cm D)*

British Willow Plate
FOVA 1900 *(3.5 cm H × 25 cm DIAM.)*

Tea Cup
FOVA 322 *(6.5 cm H × 10.5 cm DIAM.)*

TEA CUP & SAUCER

Lieutenant Charles Wilkes reported that in 1841, "Towards sunset, tea-time arrived, and we obeyed the summons of the bell, when we were introduced to several of the gentlemen of the establishment; we met in a large hall, with a long table spread with an abundance of good fare." Tea drinking was a popular activity at Fort Vancouver, not just among the elite but also among the people of the village. This tea-cup represents both the spread of Asian form and design to the West and the globalization of the custom of drinking tea. While tea drinking dates back over five thousand years in China, it is relatively new to the rest of the world. Tea drinking began in Europe during the 1600s, when tea was very rare and expensive, much like Chinese porcelain. Portuguese and Dutch companies were the earliest tea traders. The British East India Company did not capitalize on tea's popularity until the mid-1700s. By forcing the production of opium in India in order to exchange it for tea in China—the trilateral trade system—the East India Company saved itself from having to exchange coin for tea, thus making its business extremely profitable. The tea-for-opium trade eventually led to the Opium Wars of the mid-nineteenth century, and to the East India Company's monopoly on the tea trade. A teacup from Fort Vancouver therefore is tied to an immense global process that changed the Northwest as it changed the world.

Saucer
FOVA 36099 *(3.5 cm H × 17.5 cm DIAM.)*

CORAL & ENGLISH BRICK WITH CORAL MORTAR

These two artifacts exemplify globalization at Fort Vancouver. The coral is from Hawaii and was used to make mortar for the brick Powder Magazine and chimneys of the Hudson's Bay Company buildings. This brick was made in England. Together, these two objects represent the long sea journey of supplies from London to Vancouver. George Simpson wrote about the other Hawaiian import, human labor, when he visited the islands in 1841: "About a thousand males in the very prime of life are estimated annually to leave the islands, some going to California, others to the Columbia, and many on long and dangerous voyages, particularly in whaling vessels, while a number of them are said to be permanently lost to their country, either dying during their engagements, or settling in other parts of the world."

English Brick with Coral Mortar
FOVA 7833 (11.5 CM H × 17 CM W × 7.5 CM D)

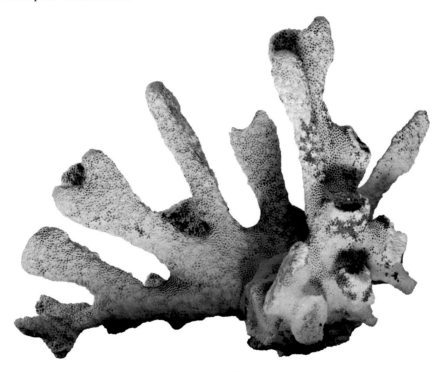

Coral
FOVA 9879 (10 CM H × 19 CM W × 14 CM D)

CHINESE & JAPANESE PORCELAIN

These beautiful porcelain objects represent two different eras of Asian imports at Fort Vancouver. The object on the bottom is a Japanese porcelain teapot recovered from a former pond in the village area that became a trash dump for the U.S. Army. The object on the top is a Chinese Ginger Jar bearing design themes similar to those seen on modern Chinese imports as well as Spode transfer-printed wares. Pots like these have been produced in China for hundreds of years, which makes dating such objects challenging unless they appear in a context with finite dates, such as at Fort Vancouver. These ceramics illustrate the way trade and trading partners change according to prevailing governments' foreign policy.

Chinese Ginger Jar
FOVA 32826 (16 CM H × 15 CM DIAM.)

Japanese Teapot
FOVA 21896 (11.5 CM H × 14 CM W × 19 CM D)

PHOENIX BUTTONS

These uniform buttons are interesting international artifacts. They were made in England for King Christophe of Haiti. After Christophe's suicide in 1820, these buttons were put on the open market and many ended up in the northwestern United States, particularly at fur trade and Indian sites along the Columbia River. Emory Strong hypothesized that they entered the lower Columbia River in the possession of Nathanial Wyeth, an American trader who in 1832 and 1834 challenged the Hudson's Bay Company's dominance in the fur trade. McLoughlin wrote: "We opposed him [Wyeth] as much as was Necessary. We had and still have Mr. Ermatinger in the Flat head Country and Mr. McKay in the Snake Country and they opposed our opponents so Effectually that they are Receding from us...we may be certain Wyeths Losses are Great, and though he still keeps up Fort Hall yet he has very few Goods." McLoughlin later bought out Wyeth's stock of goods and purchased Fort Hall for the Hudson's Bay Company. While Wyeth's American venture failed, these buttons may provide a tangible record of his attempt as well as a tie to global political events.

Phoenix Buttons
FOVA 10930 (1.5 CM DIAM.),
10931 (1 CM H × 1.5 CM DIAM.),
10932 (1 CM H × 1.5 CM DIAM.),
and 10933 (2.5 CM DIAM.)

HEALTH

Germs, Food, and Medicine

◆ *Heidi K. Pierson*

WHEN FORT VANCOUVER was established in 1825, both Euro-American and indigenous cultures had theories of disease that were very different from those held in medicine today. In Europe and America, germ theory had not yet been developed, and it was believed that most ailments were caused by excessive fluids and "ill humors" in the body, which were treated by bloodletting and purging techniques. Indians relied mainly on shamans, herbal medicine, and sweating to maintain health and remove illnesses; synthetic medicines were not yet available. Practices we consider unhealthful today, particularly drinking alcohol and smoking tobacco, were not only tolerated, but in some cases were thought of as healthful.

In the Pacific Northwest, epidemics were a constant threat to the entire population, though different subgroups had differing levels of susceptibility and various preferred treatments. During the 1830s, malaria—referred to as "intermittent fever" or "fever and ague"—swept through the lower Columbia River Basin, afflicting both Europeans and Indians. Indians were highly susceptible to the disease, and their population dropped by an estimated 88 percent. Europeans were also afflicted in great numbers, but their mortality rate was much lower. For several years during the peak fever season, so many Hudson's Bay Company employees were sick that the fort's business came to a standstill. Two new doctors were requested from London to help deal with the outbreaks, and the Company sent Drs. William Fraser Tolmie and Meredith Gairdner. Dr. Gairdner erected a hospital in the summer of 1833. Located about six hundred yards southwest of the fort, it was probably intended for inhabitants of the village and local Indians, while officers and their families were treated in their quarters. Treatment involved cleansing the air with smoke, bloodletting, purging, and finally restoring the body with tonics. Herbal remedies included quinine (from the Cinchona tree), dogwood bark, willow bark, and horse chestnut.

The doctor's main practice likely took place either in the Bachelors' Quarters or attached to the Indian Trade Shop, with space divided into a surgery and dispensary. In addition to caring for the families of Fort Vancouver, the doctor treated Indians free of charge and local American settlers for a fee. The presence of a doctor on the frontier was part of what made Fort Vancouver an attractive place. Dr. Forbes Barclay was stationed at the fur trade post during its period of peak population and activity in the 1840s.

Fort Vancouver had not only a staff physician but also an agricultural program that could supply the fort's dependents with many types of fresh food and medicinal herbs, an important feature for maintaining health. Alongside historic documents, artifacts—especially domestic debris and soil samples from the garden area—can enhance our understanding of health and diet in the past.

The Lower Columbia River was (and is) a rich area that provided its inhabitants with an incredibly diverse diet. Before European and American contact, what is now the Portland-Vancouver basin provided abundant food that was able to support year-round villages and seasonal visitors with resources such as camas and wapato (starchy root vegetables), berries, salmon, deer, elk, and fowl. By the mid-1840s, Fort Vancouver had developed a large farming operation with numerous crops, orchards, cattle, sheep, hogs, a salmon-packing operation, and even a formal garden. Given its remoteness from England, self-sufficiency was of paramount importance. According to many written accounts, guests of the fort were often treated to large meals, no doubt facilitated by the variety of fruits, vegetables, and grains growing nearby. Also grown in the garden were medicinal herbs for use, presumably, by the fort's physician. The variety and abundance of foods greatly facilitated the survival of American immigrants, many of whom would have starved without the assistance of Chief Factor McLoughlin.

While officers and their families were eating well, most employees subsisted on much simpler fare. Company employees received basic rations: dried peas, bread, salmon, occasionally salt beef, and alcohol (a small yearly ration). Rations were meant to feed only one person two meals per day and were supplemented by hunting, gardening small plots, and the gathering of native plants by women, who were usually members of local tribes.

Fever epidemics notwithstanding, things were probably much better for the employees of the Hudson's Bay Company than they were for the enlisted men of the U.S. Army. When the Army established its post here in 1849, the food was notoriously bad. The usual daily ration consisted of meat, flour, coffee, beans, and salt, with little variation. One innovation of the mid-nineteenth century was the use of desiccated vegetables, in the form of dried sheets later reconstituted, to supplement the diet. Unfortunately, these vegetables had a reputation for looking horrible and tasting worse, earning them the nickname "desecrated vegetables." At Vancouver Barracks, the soldiers were fortunate enough to have access to a sutler's store. The sutler provided a variety of goods and foodstuffs for those who could afford to supplement their rations.

Food in the Army improved over time, following general trends in agriculture, science, and industry. During the eighteenth and nineteenth centuries, soldiers cooked for themselves in the field and rotated kitchen duties at the post, which no doubt contributed to the low quality of the food. The office of uniformed cook was eventually created and recognized by an increase in rank and pay. By the early twentieth century, cooks and bakers schools had been established to train cooks to a single standard throughout the Army.

While the Hudson's Bay Company doctor took care of everyone until the last doctor decamped in 1859, the U.S. Army only treated soldiers and their dependents. In 1858, a new two-story military hospital was built on the east side of the parade ground. That same year, the

Sisters of Providence—led by Mother Joseph—established St. Joseph's Hospital at St. James Mission, adjacent to the military post. In the beginning, the hospital was housed in a portion of a sixteen-by-twenty foot structure, sharing space with a bakery. During the following decades, the hospital grew and eventually moved to its current location on Mill Plain Boulevard (now the Southwest Washington Medical Center). The organization created by Mother Joseph grew into the Providence health care system.

The post hospital also expanded. In 1903 or 1904 a third, state-of-the-art hospital building was erected. The new hospital incorporated all of the latest ideas about medicine, including germ theory, and it is significant that it was built with plans designed not by the Quartermaster's Office (as was usual) but by the Surgeon General's Office. It was designed according to a sanatorium layout, with open rooms meant to allow fresh air to circulate and sunlight to reach the rooms, creating a healthful atmosphere for patients. In addition, the new hospital was designed to be easy to clean and disinfect, with no interior moldings or other horizontal architectural elements that could act as a breeding ground for germs. It even featured an X-ray room.

During World War I, the post hospital responded to several crises. In addition to treating and rehabilitating soldiers returning from the Front, the hospital served troops from the Spruce Production Division and those infected with influenza during the epidemic of 1918. Thousands of soldiers were needed to work both at logging camps throughout the Northwest and in the main mill at Vancouver. High accident rates in the camps and an influenza outbreak among the "tent city" that housed workers at the mill meant a heavy burden for the overloaded post hospital. Even though temporary beds had to be set up in corridors and other free space, the staff at the hospital was able to handle the situation. The epidemic killed 18 million people worldwide, but medical records show that relatively few died at the post. The post hospital was operational until 1946 and remains standing to this day.

During the next war, the Kaiser Company established shipyards at Vancouver. Along with housing, Kaiser offered its employees health and child care, somewhat revolutionary concepts for the 1940s. The small corporate hospital on a bluff overlooking the Vancouver yard eventually grew into the Kaiser Permanente health care system.

Through the history of Fort Vancouver and Vancouver Barracks, one can trace several medical milestones. Though most people here today have easy access to pharmacies, preventive care, and nutritious foods, these are modern benefits. A staff physician trained in Scotland and a nutritious, varied diet were cutting-edge medical care for a frontier trading post. The military hospitals here were top-of-the-line institutions at the time of their establishment. Objects within the museum collection offer a unique view of medical traditions over time, and also of an evolving diet.

TOBACCO PIPE STEMS

Tobacco pipe fragments like these are found all over Fort Vancouver and its environs. Tobacco had been in common use throughout the Americas for centuries but truly became a worldwide phenomenon during the Age of Exploration. By the mid sixteenth century, tobacco was hailed as a medicinal herb: Nicolas Bautista Monardes, a Spanish physician—considered one of the founders of experimental pharmacology—named thirty-six medicinal uses for tobacco. Herbalists all over Spain began to grow the plant, and by the late sixteenth century, tobacco was used medicinally all over Europe. Tobacco smoking reached widespread popularity during the seventeenth century, "The Great Age of the Pipe," but also stirred controversy. The Pope banned smoking in holy places, and the Mongolian Emperor made tobacco smoking punishable by death. Needless to say, smoking was still a popular activity during the nineteenth century, and while it remained controversial even then, it was not until the twentieth century that the ill effects of tobacco were universally acknowledged.

At Hudson's Bay Company establishments, most individuals smoked, and contemporary descriptions of their quarters frequently mention smoke-filled interiors. As with many archaeological artifacts, the research potential of tobacco pipes is seen in their distribution across the site rather than in each individual object. Densities of pipe stem fragments in a single location, for example adjacent to the Sale Shop, indicate a "waiting area" where customers congregated prior to going inside; this also suggests the original position of an entrance. The presence or lack of tobacco pipes can even reflect past behaviors: the almost complete absence of pipe fragments near the Powder Magazine implies that smoking near the stocks of gunpowder was prohibited (quite sensibly).

The Indian and Métis wives of employees were also described as having a habit of smoking, even though it was often considered unladylike by their husbands. Pierre Pambrun, a Chief Trader with the Company, even offered his wife diamond earrings if she would give up her pipe—to no avail.

Tobacco Pipe Stems
FOVA 191
(fragments of varying sizes)

SURGICAL INSTRUMENTS

In 1830, McLoughlin wrote: "The Intermitting Fever (for the first time since the trade of this Department was Established) has appeared at this place and carried off three fourths of the Indn. [Indian] population in our vicinity: at present there are fifty two of our people on the sick list." Two years later, the Hudson's Bay Company sent Drs. Tolmie and Gairdner to Fort Vancouver.

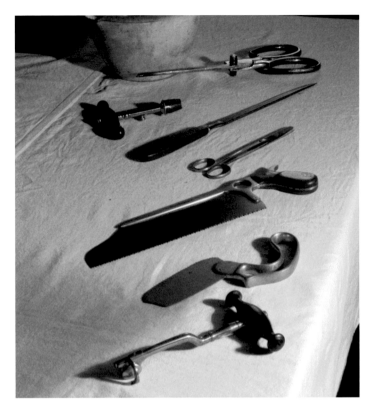

These types of surgical instruments, antiques acquired to furnish the surgery at Fort Vancouver, are similar to those described by Tolmie, who used such tools for bloodletting, amputation, and other types of surgery. Two days after his arrival at Fort Vancouver Tolmie wrote: "There is a very excellent supply of surgical instruments—an Amputating, two trephining, two eye instruments, a lithotomy & a cupping case, besides two midwifery forceps & a multitude of catheters, flexible and silver sounds bougies, bandages, probangs, tooth forceps &c. not yet put in order." The use of bleeding to treat intermittent fever (malaria) was recorded by Tolmie in 1832: "The fever has appeared in the piquets [stockade]—the Dr. [McLoughlin], his son & daughter being laid up with it, bleeding has been tried in the cold stage of the Dr's case & a paroxysm has not since returned, altho' nausea & debility remain." Four days later, near present-day Kalama, Washington, he noted "the site of an indian village, which a few years ago contained two or three hundred inhabitants, but at present only its superior verdure distinguished the spot from the surrounding country. Intermittent fever which has almost depopulated Columbia R. of the aborigines, committed its fullest ravages & nearly exterminated the villagers, the few survivors deserting a spot where the pestilence seemed most terribly to wreck its vengeance."

SERVING DISHES

The fort's farms, gardens, and dairies provided officers, their families, and guests with a wide variety of fresh foods. Such a diet was rare on the frontier and depended greatly on the labor of Indian, Hawaiian, and other workers. The journal of Narcissa Whitman describes a typical dinner at the Chief Factor's House:

> *Sept. 23, 1836 Vancouver:* There is such a variety I know not where to begin.... First we are *always* treated to a dish of soup, which is very good. Every kind of vegetable in use is taken & choped fine & put into water with a little rice and boiled to a soup. The taumatoes are a promanant article. Usually some fowl meat duck or any kind, is cut fine & added if it has been roasted once it is just as good, (so the cook says) they spiced to taste. After our soup dishes are removed, then comes a variety of meats, to prove our tastes. After selecting & tasting, change plates & try another if we choose, so at ever new dish, have a clean plate. Roast duck is an every day dish, boiled pork, tripe, & sometimes trotter, fresh Salmon or Sturgeon, yea to numerous to mention. When these are set aside A rice pudding or an apple pie is next introduced. After this melons next make their appearance, some times grapes & last of all cheese, bread or biscuit & butter is produced to complet the whole.

The array of serving dishes excavated from within the fort site speaks not only to the nutritious and varied diet enjoyed by the upper classes but also to the European dining traditions that were continued in the Oregon Country. Large, expensive hollowware ceramics, like the platter and strainer, tureen, and vegetable dish shown here, are almost always associated with the Chief Factor's House rather than village houses.

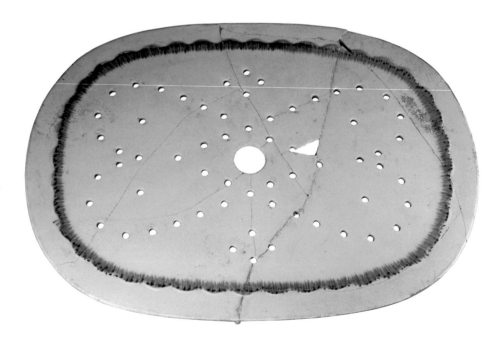

Strainer
FOVA 90 (24 cm H × 33.5 cm W × 2 cm D)

Platter
FOVA 36380 (33 cm H × 44 cm W × 5 cm D)

Vegetable Dish
FOVA 2101 (22 cm H × 26 cm W × 5.5 cm D)

Tureen
FOVA 2185 (17 cm H × 29.5 cm W × 28 cm D)

GARDENS

Fort Vancouver gardens.
Courtesy of the National Park Service. Photo by Gregory P. Shine.

For the upper classes at least, the formal gardens at Fort Vancouver offered not only healthful produce but also a beautiful place to walk and rest. It was a stark contrast to the harsh areas employees or visitors may have experienced elsewhere in the West. Another entry in Narcissa Whitman's journal recounts:

> *September 12 1836, Vancouver:* Soon after we were Introduced to Mrs. McLaughlin & Mrs. Douglas, both natives of this country (half breed). After chatting a little we were invited to walk in the garden. And what a delightful place this. What a contrast this to the barren sand plains through which we had so recently passed. Here we find fruit of every description. Apples peaches grapes. Pear plum & Fig trees in abundance. Cucumbers melons beans peas cabbage, taumatoes, & every kind of vegitable, to numerous to be mentioned. Every part is neat & tastefully arranged fine walks, eich side lined with strawberry vines. On the opposite end of the garden is a good Summer house covered with grape vines.

Microartifacts, those less than one millimeter in size, are often overlooked in the archaeological record. Pollen and phytoliths (the hard parts of plants), however, offer a wealth of information about early agricultural practices, diet, and, more indirectly, health.

BOTTLES

Before the twentieth century, the U.S. Army relied on civilian contractors, known as sutlers, to provision troops with goods and supplemental foodstuffs. The sutler paid a fee to set up shop and was regulated by Army officers to prevent him from overcharging the soldiers. The sutler was able to supply goods such as spices and herbs, camphor, bicarbonate of soda, coffee, tea, cans of lobsters, sardines, oysters, cheese, flour, cornmeal, yeast, casks of brandy, cases of cider, cigars, clay pipes, molasses, boots, women's and boys' shoes, wool socks, bags of shot, a keg of powder in canisters, candles, and much more. Alcoholic beverages were also noted products at sutlers' stores; however, it is interesting that a General Order of September 29, 1849, restricted sutlers from "keeping ardent spirits or other intoxicating drinks." Evidently, the General Order did little to thwart the consumption of alcohol at the sutler's store: these well-preserved alcohol bottles were found in the sutler's store privy. These whole bottles represent a range of types, from alcohol to toiletry bottles. From left to right: medicinal Jamaica ginger bottle (1844–1865), made in New York; quart-sized liquor or brandy bottle; medicine bottle; liquor case bottle with chamfered corners; medicine bottle; castor oil or florida water (eau de toilette) bottle.

Bottles FOVA-3024, Lot 807 Spec 1 (37.84 mm H × 1903 mm DIAM.),
Lot 808 Spec 1 (152 mm H × 67.8 mm DIAM.), Lot 809 Spec 1 (265 mm H × 59 mm DIAM.),
Lot 810 Spec 1 (190 mm H × 17.2 mm DIAM.), Lot 811 Spec 1 (24 mm H × 15.49 mm DIAM.),
and Lot 812 Spec 1 (145 mm H × 55.93 mm W × 31.23 mm D)

ALCOHOL BOTTLES

One constant in archaeology at Fort Vancouver is the presence of alcohol bottles. Like tobacco pipes, they are distributed throughout the site and reflect the almost complete acceptance of responsible alcohol consumption at both the fur trade and military posts. It should be noted, however, that excessive consumption was not tolerated; Hudson's Bay Company employees could be punished with house arrest and loss of pay, or even flogging, for drunkenness. There were also serious consequences for U.S. Army soldiers who over-consumed. Even though his own employees received rations of rum, McLoughlin did not support alcohol trade to Indians and tried to discourage American traders from the practice.

Fort Vancouver imported several types of alcohol, including beer, wine, champagne, rum, and brandy. The preferred wine was Chateau Margaux, still in existence and now a famous and expensive variety. Though Vancouver Barracks officially did not supply alcohol, it was available from the sutler on the post as well as in the taverns that clustered on the closest edge of town. Henry Weinhard's brewery first started in Vancouver in 1857, and Lucky Lager Brewery operated here from 1939 (as Interstate Brewery Company) until 1985.

These photos show a few of the different types of alcohol bottles found at this site. Stoneware bottles for "Read's India Pale Ale," wine bottles, and rum or brandy bottles have been found all across Fort Vancouver. The Lucky Lager beer bottle and Old Cellar whiskey bottle were recovered from underneath a Vancouver Barracks building.

Wine Bottle
FOVA 559 (25 CM H
× 6 CM DIAM.)

Rum or Brandy Bottle
FOVA 9638 (29.21 CM H
× 7.62 CM DIAM.)

Lucky Lager Bottle
FOVA 160038
(24 CM H)

Old Cellar Whiskey
Bottle
FOVA 160040
(21 CM H)

Read's India Pale Ale Bottles
FOVA 15117 (25.4 CM H × 8.89 CM DIAM.),
10436 (12 CM H × 9 CM DIAM.),
and 48635 (11.5 CM H × 8.5 CM DIAM.)

FISH VERTEBRA & COW BONE

Though employees of the Hudson's Bay Company received rations, the food was meant to feed a single male and was not enough to support family members. As a result, many employees had to supplement by tending small personal gardens, hunting, fishing, and gathering plants. Remains of meals left in the archaeological record offer evidence of diet; for example, fish vertebra are a fairly common sight during village excavations, reflecting the consumption of salmon and other Columbia River catches.

Fort Vancouver had several thousand head of livestock, including cattle, sheep, and pigs. Eating them was forbidden during the early years of the farm enterprise, and they were left to multiply in order to build up the herd. Later, the meat was still off-limits to most employees, as beef especially became a profitable export from the Oregon Country.

In contrast, one of the first acts of the U.S. Army's Quartermaster—as Vancouver Barracks was being established in 1849 and 1850—was to bring in cattle to feed the troops. This foreleg bone with butchery marks was found during excavations at the site of the post's earliest kitchen, on the west end of what later became the parade ground.

Fish Vertebra
FOVA 17845 (3 cm L × 4 cm W × 1 cm D)

Cow Bone
FOVA 17979 (20 cm L × 9 cm W × 5 cm D)

CHAMBER POTS & TOILET

Chamber pots illustrate fundamental differences in the ways people took care of their sanitary concerns. Well into the nineteenth century, and indeed into the twentieth, it was commonplace for most people to use the combination of an outhouse and, at night, a chamber pot. Among the upper classes, servants rather than users would empty the pots. This was probably true inside Fort Vancouver, the chore a duty of the stewards. Fur trade–era chamber pots shown on this page include handpainted cottageware, mochaware, and an Alhambra transferprinted pattern on earthenware. Chamber pots are rarely found in the village and perhaps reflect the occupants' more casual approach to hygiene.

Earthenware Chamber Pot
FOVA 9677 (Pot: 13 cm H × 23 cm DIAM.;
Lid: 7 cm H × 21.5 cm DIAM.;
Pot with lid: 20 cm H × 23 cm DIAM.)

Cottageware Chamber Pot
FOVA 654 (Pot: 14 cm H × 22 cm DIAM.;
Lid: 5.5 cm H × 22.5 cm DIAM.;
Pot with lid: 19.5 cm H × 22.5 cm DIAM.)

Mochaware Chamber Pot
FOVA 66 (13.5 cm H × 26 cm W × 23 cm DIAM.)

The white, undecorated ironstone chamber pot is from the U.S. Army era. An early cream-ware chamber pot, with the Arms of the United States of America on one side and a compass rose on the other, dates to before 1820 and may have been an heirloom piece owned by someone at Vancouver Barracks. It was made in Liverpool, England, but its patriotic decoration suggests it was meant for the American market.

Most early toilets were modeled after the chamber pot, and many were as elaborately decorated. The first toilets in the Oregon Country were likely those at Vancouver Barracks; the region's first indoor plumbing for a bathroom was in one of the officer's quarters on Officers' Row. This toilet was unearthed in a World War I–era trash deposit and dates to the late nineteenth century.

Chamber Pot
FOVA 131159 (15 CM H × 22 CM DIAM.)

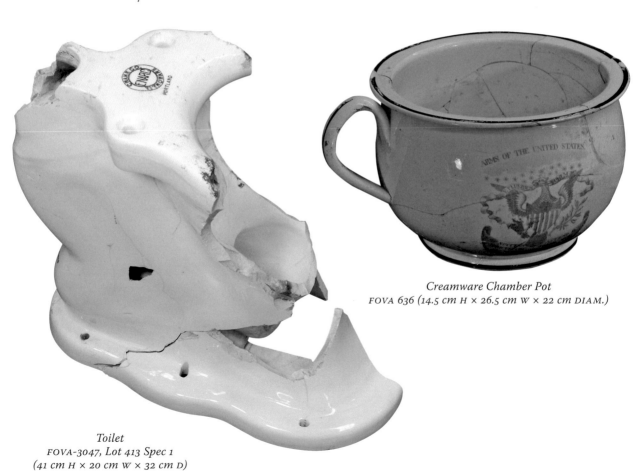

Toilet
FOVA-3047, Lot 413 Spec 1
(41 CM H × 20 CM W × 32 CM D)

Creamware Chamber Pot
FOVA 636 (14.5 CM H × 26.5 CM W × 22 CM DIAM.)

TOOTH POWDER JAR, TOOTHBRUSH, & BEAR GREASE JAR

As with chamber pots, certain forms of personal hygiene seem to be prevalent only among the officers and their families at Fort Vancouver. All of these items were found within the fort stockade. The bone toothbrush would have been used with cherry-flavored tooth powder. The bear grease was for use on hair.

Tooth Powder Jar
FOVA 233 *(2 cm H × 8 cm DIAM.)*

Toothbrush
FOVA 592 *(15 cm L × 1.2 cm W × 1.5 cm D)*

Bear Grease Jar
FOVA 10423 *(1.5 cm H × 7.5 cm DIAM.)*

THE PARK TODAY

◈ *Gregory P. Shine*

AT THE END of the classic film *Raiders of the Lost Ark*, one of the world's most fabled artifacts, the Ark of the Covenant, meets a rather inauspicious end. Rather than being shared with the world, it is unceremoniously sealed in a nondescript wooden crate, which is stamped "Top Secret" and wheeled into a vast federal warehouse where it is quickly lost to the eye amid thousands of identical boxes. Although a fictional account, the scene nonetheless represents a popular perception of the fate of many archaeological artifacts.

Luckily, this is not the case with the collections at Fort Vancouver. In fact, this movie scene represents the exact opposite of the way artifacts are valued and utilized in the park. On a daily basis, the items in the park's collections help the National Park Service better interpret the site and its history. From programs to publications to online exhibits to the reconstructed fort itself, the treasures of Fort Vancouver play a special role every day. They demonstrate to the public that although archaeology is used to study the past, it is relevant to the modern world.

One of the highlights of any visit to Fort Vancouver is a walk around the reconstructed fur trade-era fort. Its tall wooden palisade and bastion bristling with cannon is one of the Pacific Northwest's most recognizable icons. Few people realize that the presence of the reconstructed stockade and its accompanying buildings is due largely to the archaeological record, those artifacts still underground (known as *in situ*) as well as many of the items preserved in the park's collection.

All of the buildings within the Hudson's Bay Company stockade and village are modern reconstructions based on meticulous historical and archaeological research. Reconstruction efforts are currently focusing on the village area, above, where roads, fencelines, and two houses begin to give visitors a sense of this community. The Counting House, right, shown here during construction, was reconstructed in 2003, while the Jail (behind) was reconstructed in 2001. The first reconstructed feature was the north wall of the stockade (background), which was reconstructed in 1966. Courtesy of the National Park Service. Photos by Gregory P. Shine.

Reconstruction of historic buildings and landscapes is rare in units of the National Park System, and for significant reasons. As the steward of our nation's history, the National Park Service holds as a basic principle that anything of historical appearance that is presented to the public will be either an authentic survival from the past or an accurate representation of what once existed. Given this philosophy, the National Park Service will usually not undertake the reconstruction of absent resources or features. In certain cases, when critical elements are met, the National Park Service will reconstruct now-absent features such as buildings. For example, any reconstruction must occur in an original location. In addition, significant data must exist to support an accurate reconstruction and data must be substantiated by site-specific documentary or physical evidence.

This presented a particular challenge in the early days of Fort Vancouver's establishment as a National Historic Site. The original

Excavators Rod Smith and Rex Gerald showing archaeological remains exposed during the 1950 National Park Service excavations to a young visitor. The top of a privy pit ("Trash Pit 6") and two different iterations of the 1834–1845 stockade wall are shown. The privy pit was directly behind the Priest's House kitchen, which was also used as a Hawaiian church by William Kalehelehe. Like most of the privy pits, it contained abundant artifacts. The stockade posts showed precisely where the walls of the stockade were built, repaired, or replaced. Courtesy of the National Park Service.

Hudson's Bay Company stockade, along with most of the buildings, had fallen into disrepair and burned in the 1860s. Subsequently, the U.S. Army actively used the site, adapting the landscape and adding significant structures. When the centennial of the fort's construction dawned in the 1920s, many knew of the fort's historic presence, but its original location was unknown until archaeological excavations in 1947 identified features and artifacts that defined the location of the fort and literally uncovered a treasure trove of physical evidence.

Reconstruction at Fort Vancouver is a vital, ongoing process that is indelibly linked to—and driven by—the site's archaeological excavations and studies. Without these critical discoveries and their contribution to the historical record, it is unlikely that the fort would be in existence today; nor would future reconstructions inside the stockade walls, such as the Powder Magazine and Sale Shop, and outside the walls in the village and wharf areas, bc available for the public to enjoy.

The contribution of the artifacts in the park's collection is in no way limited to reconstructing historical buildings. The artifacts, books,

and maps in the collection are tangible links to the past that staff use through tours, programs, printed materials, exhibits, and electronic media to help connect visitors to the site's history.

One of the most valuable ways archaeological artifacts and other collections items aid historians and archaeologists is in helping them tell a more complete story. The documentary record—in the form of letters, ledgers, journals, drawings, maps, and photographs—provides a wealth of detail about the fort's administration and those responsible for it, the gentleman class. The ability to read and write has historically excluded the stories of many working class people, leaving a gap in the nation's record of its past. At Fort Vancouver, in comparison to the wealth of insight documents provide into the lives of the officers and clerks, there is painfully little that speaks to the lives of the majority of people who lived at the fort, the workers. This is rather unexpected, for members of the working class far outnumbered the gentleman class at Fort Vancouver, often by about ten to one. Fortunately, this is where the fort's archaeological treasures prove of tremendous value.

The fire hearth and post holes visible in this image of the 2003 excavation of the House 5 site in the village offer insight into working class life in the village that complements the historical record and expands our understanding of the site. Courtesy of the National Park Service. Photo by Doug Wilson.

The park's immersive, hands-on education programs combine evidence from the historical and archaeological records to help young visitors develop their own, personal understanding of the site and its significance. Courtesy of the National Park Service. Photo by Michael Liang.

Recent excavations in the village, just to the west of the stockade, help bring the stories of the fort's working class to life. Artifacts such as hearth stones, beads, pipes, tools, window glass, pottery sherds, and animal bones tell us much about the economy and daily life of these diverse Company employees and their families.

By rediscovering artifacts in areas such as the village, the collection helps expand the site's themes and forge new dimensions to the site's identity—dimensions that sustain and herald the site's historic role as a community gathering place. For example, the diversity of the workforce, and the way individuals operated within it, echoes our own increasingly diverse communities. The National Park Service advises parks *to be relevant or be a relic*, and the park staff recognizes that building connections between the collection and park events is a prime way to ensure relevance. The collection helps inform and broaden the scope of special events, such as the Children's Culture Parade, an annual celebration of world culture and tradition that brings hundreds of elementary school children to the park, and the Fourth of July celebration, an event that attracts over 60,000 visitors each year. In turn, the

events help disseminate information about the park and the collection while simultaneously augmenting the site's role as a place for the community to meet and interact.

The fort's artifacts also greatly improve the accuracy of the stories being told, including those shared through living history and costumed interpretation. At the fort's Blacksmith Shop, staff and volunteers in authentic costume use techniques and materials from the fort's heyday to interpret the lives of critically important Company employees. While the image of a blacksmith often conjures thoughts of shoeing horses, the fort's blacksmiths demonstrate that the job could be quite different. The blacksmiths can often be observed hammering away at a beaver trap or a trade axe, items they are able to replicate from original examples in the collection. A historic inventory document may list a beaver trap, but to have several archaeological examples—in various states of manufacture—provides an opportunity for the blacksmiths to imitate the technology of the past, using many of the same materials and procedures in the same location as their predecessors did almost two centuries ago.

Information about the lives of the Company's working class employees culled, in part, from artifacts in the park's collection helps inform special events onsite, such as the park's annual Brigade Encampment. Courtesy of the National Park Service. Photo by Robert Holcomb.

Today, Fort Vancouver National Historic Site encompasses 209 acres of green space in the middle of a major urban center. Although the park's collections include over two million artifacts, less than twenty percent of the park's acreage has been formally excavated by archaeologists. Courtesy of the National Park Service. Photo by Gregory P. Shine.

While the artifacts recovered through archaeology are the site's most prominent resource, there are also a number of other treasures in the collection that help bring voice to long-silenced stories. Handcrafted quilts and delicate women's dresses that once "tripped the light fantastic" at balls on Officers' Row help us better understand the important role women played throughout the post's history. Without these donated collection items, many of these stories might not be told; certainly, they could not be told as compellingly.

Despite a collection of over two million artifacts, only a small percentage of the park grounds has been excavated and studied. The wealth of artifacts still underground and unexplored, as well as the analysis of many of the artifacts recently excavated, has led to one of the most exciting new programs in the nation. In 2004, the National Park Service established the Northwest Cultural Resources Institute (NCRI), based at Fort Vancouver. The NCRI is a cooperative partnership dedicated to facilitating research and educational activities relating to the cultural resources of the area. The foundations of the NCRI include the renowned archaeological collection, the archaeological resources remaining *in situ*, and the extant historic architecture. These form an unparalleled opportunity for researchers, students, and members of the public to study within the fields of archaeology, history, curation and collections management, museum studies, preservation, and historic architecture, using national parks as laboratories.

Whether it is excavating and describing a long-lost village house or developing a living-history program for the public, the collections of Fort Vancouver play a vital role in inspiring interest, provoking thought, stimulating new analysis, and fostering stewardship in our future educators and experts—and in the visiting public. The NCRI demonstrates the efficacy and relevance of the fort's treasures and ensures public access for generations of study and analysis. An alternative scene from *Raiders of the Lost Ark* featuring fictional archaeologist Dr. Belloq better exemplifies the value of artifacts. "We are simply passing through history," he remarks. "These artifacts...these *are* history." Nowhere is this truth better exemplified than at Fort Vancouver.

WHY COLLECTIONS MATTER

◈ *Tracy A. Fortmann*

Why do we care for this place?

It is a magnificent place, where the sun rises over the shoulders of Mount Hood and shines down on the mighty Columbia River, where prairie lands merge into fir forest. This region has beckoned people for thousands of years.

Many types of people—indigenous groups, American settlers, fur trappers, soldiers, Hawaiian workers, Chinese domestic servants— were both emboldened by this place and tested by it. The history is rich, complicated, compelling, difficult, and in many ways, highly rewarding. As a part of the National Park Service, we are the caretakers of this site. As thoughtful stewards, we have a responsibility to look to the past for important direction and insight. Tangible pieces of our past have been gathered to become the Fort Vancouver museum collection, a key part of the archaeological and historical record of the Pacific Northwest.

Globalization and *Technology* shaped this place, from its indigenous beginnings through the European fur trade, to the fledging U.S. military post and, finally, to a major, strategically important shipyard installation that built Liberty Ships during World War II. The acquisition of furs for fashion and profit forever changed the landscape of the Pacific Northwest, and there is no question that the fur-desert policy had tremendous environmental repercussions. In many respects, the Pacific Northwest is what it is today because of the decisions that led to these forces of change.

In the section *Health*, we learn that in just a few short years,

University students utilize the Fort Vancouver collections for teaching and research. Elizabeth Horton, a doctoral candidate in archaeology at Washington State University, and Meagan Huff, an NPS Museum Technician, explain historical maps from the museum archives to a public history class from Portland State University. Courtesy of the National Park Service. Photo by Robert Holcomb.

thousands of Indians died due to introduced pathogens. As a society today, we are all facing new and evolving virulent diseases. The severe, widespread, and indiscriminate hand of epidemics is as real and devastating today as it was then. Our reaction to health challenges is reflected in our diet, our medicine, and other aspects of our cultural ways of life that impact human health. The objects from Fort Vancouver tell that story of changing perspectives and responses to human health issues.

Is our future different from our past? Do not our actions today help determine our future? As a people, we hopefully will continue to look for clues in the tangible objects left behind, and critically examine history in order to learn from our past to make the best possible decisions for today and tomorrow.

Unfortunately, for many, the information embedded in museum collections is not well understood, and those who manage them are unknown. I suspect that the title Curator conjures up images of odd-looking scientist-types, wearing thick-framed glasses and hunched

intently over objects in a dark catacomb of seemingly endless rows of nondescript drawers and filing systems. Certainly, nothing could be farther from the truth with regard to collections here at this urban national park. Fort Vancouver is a living laboratory with a dynamic educational program. We have a vibrant, active curatorial facility in which National Park Service professionals promote the study of cultural resources and ensure that the collections are available to researchers, students, and the general public. A vital component of our stewardship responsibilities is sharing the collection so many people, in varying degrees, can study it and learn. Archaeological and historical collections are tangible pieces of our past. They are often crucial pieces to a historical puzzle, providing information that cannot be gleaned elsewhere. Through these collections, opportunities to learn about people, places, and stories present themselves. Not just the stories of those who are renowned but also those who are less known and for which there is little or no information in the written record. The section *Identity* frankly speaks to those universal aspects of human

The climate-controlled curation facility at Fort Vancouver, which is open for public visits and educational tours, houses most of the two million objects in the park's collection, as well as collections from several other national parks. Courtesy of the National Park Service.

Historic buildings—including these barracks buildings dating from the early twentieth century—play an important role in defining the cultural landscape of the site. Preservation of these and other historic resources is an important part of the National Park Service mission. Courtesy of the National Park Service.

beings. Be it by nature or nurture, or a combination of the two, we human beings collect things. There is a wide range in what we choose to collect, but we all do it in some form. Ultimately, extensive collections such as the ones we protect and preserve at Fort Vancouver have far-reaching value to all of us.

We are fortunate that Fort Vancouver is very intact. It includes sites, historic structures and cultural landscapes. Where buildings, transportation routes, or heritage trees have been lost, they have been replaced with painstakingly developed reconstructions and innovative constructs, such as the landbridge that leads visitors from the Hudson's Bay Company village to the shores of the Columbia River. This is a place that was graced by national leaders: John McLoughlin, Oliver Otis Howard, Ulysses S. Grant, George Marshall, George Pickett, Phillip Sheridan, George Crook, John Gibbon, and Nelson Miles. Intellectually tying together what we learn from these leaders with the information we have gleaned, and will continue to obtain, from our collection regarding technology, identity, globalism, and the health of people, we can begin to make thoughtful decisions about the future. I think we all hope that as a people, as we advance, we

learn more and, with that new knowledge, make the best possible decisions—decisions based on all relevant information, gathered from all sources, including our past. Ultimately, the decisions we make will not just be what we live with but what our children and our children's children will have to live with. If we allow national parks to serve us, they can actually help us reflect on our collective past to help discover our best possible future.

Ultimately, we do care about our past. We Americans are passionate people who are focused on our past as we move united into the future. The National Park Service was created in 1916 with a mission that is straightforward: to preserve in perpetuity the nation's most special cultural and natural resources. We recognize that there are places within our country, such as Fort Vancouver, that are a part of our psyche and represent our spirit. Fort Vancouver is a place to be commemorated, celebrated, and learned from, not just by Americans today, but also by Americans for generations to come.

The Children's Cultural Parade, an annual event that brings close to 3,000 elementary school students to the site, exemplifies the park's role as a community touchstone where visitors can reconnect with people and things from the past. Courtesy of the National Park Service.

SOURCES

Note on Sources

Sources used in the preparation of this book are listed below by section.

Fort Vancouver

Ames, Kenneth M., and H. D. G. Maschner. 1999. *People of the Northwest Coast: Their Archaeology and Prehistory.* Thames and Hudson: London.

Ames, Kenneth M., Cameron M. Smith, William L. Cornett, Elizabeth A. Sobel, Stephen C. Hamilton, John Wolf, and Doria Raet. 1999. Archaeological Investigations at 45CL1 Cathlapotle (1991–1996), Ridgefield National Wildlife Refuge, Clark County, Washington: A Preliminary Report. U.S. Department of the Interior, Fish and Wildlife Service, Region 1 Cultural Resource Series Number 13.

Boyd, Robert T., and Yvonne P. Hayda. 1987. Seasonal Population Movement Along the Lower Columbia River: the Social and Ecological Context. *American Ethnologist* 14(2):309–325.

Darby, Melissa Cole. 1996. Wapato for the people: An ecological approach to understanding the American Indian use of *Sagittaria latifolia* on the lower Columbia. Master's Thesis, Portland State University: Portland, OR.

Hajda, Yvonne P. 2005. Slavery in the Greater Lower Columbia Region. *Ethnohistory* 52(3):563–588.

Hussey, John A. 1970. The Fort Vancouver Farm. Ms. on file, Fort Vancouver National Historic Site, Vancouver, WA.

McIrath, Laura. 2001. Archaeological Monitoring along East Reserve Street, Officer's Row, Vancouver Historic Reserve. Report by Archaeological Services of Clark County for the City of Vancouver. Ms. on file, Fort Vancouver National Historic Site, Vancouver, WA.

Merritt, Jane T. 1993. Administrative History: Fort Vancouver National Historic Site. National Park Service. Cultural Resources Division, Pacific Northwest Region, Seattle, WA. Ms. on file, Fort Vancouver National Historic Site, Vancouver, WA.

Moulton, Gary E., ed. 1990. *The Journals of the Lewis & Clark Expedition, Volume 6, November 2, 1805–March 22, 1806.* University of Nebraska Press: Lincoln.

———. 1991 *The Journals of the Lewis & Clark Expedition, Volume 7, March 22, 1806–June 9, 1806.* University of Nebraska Press: Lincoln.

Ross, Lester A. 1976. Fort Vancouver, 1829–1960: A historical archeological investigation of the goods imported and manufactured by the Hudson's Bay Company. Ms. on file, Fort Vancouver National Historic Site, Vancouver, WA.

Shine, Gregory P. 2006. Respite From War: Buffalo Soldiers at Vancouver Barracks, 1899–1900. *Oregon Historical Quarterly* 107(2):196–227. Oregon Historical Society: Portland.

Sinclair, Donna L. 2004. Part I, "Our Manifest Destiny Bids Fair For Fulfillment:" An Historical Overview of Vancouver Barracks, 1846–1898, with suggestions for further research. Report by the Center for Columbia River History for the National Park Service. Ms. on file, Fort Vancouver National Historic Site, Vancouver, WA.

———. 2005. Part III, Riptide on the Columbia: A Military Community Between the Wars, Vancouver, Washington and the Vancouver Historic Reserve, 1920–1942, with suggestions for further research. Report by the Center for Columbia River History for the National Park Service. Ms. on file, Fort Vancouver National Historic Site, Vancouver, WA.

Tonsfeldt, Ward. 2003. Spruce Mill Trail Brochure, edited by Elaine Dorset. Ms. on file, Fort Vancouver National Historic Site, Vancouver, WA.

Identity

Ballantyne, R.M. 1971. *Hudson bay, or, Everyday life in the wilds of North America: during six years' residence in the territories of the Hon. Hudson Bay Company.* Kraus Reprint: New York.

Blanchet, Francis Norbert. 1983. *Historical Sketches of the Catholic Church in Oregon.* Ye Galleon Press: Fairfield, WA.

Brighton, Stephen A. and Charles E. Orser. 2006. Irish Images on English Goods in the American Market: The Materialization of a Modern Irish Heritage. *Images, Representations and Heritage: Moving Beyond Modern Approaches to Archaeology,* edited by Ian Russell, 61–88. Springer: New York.

British and American Joint Commission on the Hudson's Bay and Puget's Sound Agricultural Companies Claims (BAJC). 1867. *Evidence for the United States in the Matter of the Claims of the Hudson's Bay and Puget's Sound Agricultural Companies Pending Before the British and American Joint Commission, for the Final Settlement of the Same. Letter from Isaac Ebey to Isaac Stevens.* M'Gill and Witherow: Washington, D.C.

Cromwell, Robert J. 2006. "Where Ornament and Function are So Agreeably Combined:"

Vancouver. Doctoral Dissertation, Department of Anthropology, Syracuse University, Syracuse, NY.

Jessett, Thomas E., editor. 1959. *Reports and Letters, 1836–1838, of Herbert Beaver, chaplain to the Hudson's Bay Company and missionary to the Indians at Fort Vancouver.* Champoeg Press: Portland.

Kardas, Susan. 1971. "The People Bought This and the Clatsop Became Rich:" A View of Nineteenth Century Fur Trade Relationships on the Lower Columbia between Chinookan Speakers, Whites, and Kanakas. Doctoral Dissertation, Department of Anthropology, Bryn Mawr College: Bryn Mawr, PA.

Hicks, Dan and Mary C. Beaudry, editors. 2006. *The Cambridge Companion to Historical Archaeology.* Cambridge University Press: Cambridge, U. K.

Howard, Oliver Otis. 1908. *Autobiography of Oliver Otis Howard, Major General, United States Army, Vol. I.* The Baker and Taylor Co.: New York.

Hussey, John A. 1972. Historic Structures Report: Historical Data Vol. I. Ms. on file, Fort Vancouver National Historic Site, Vancouver, WA.

Hussey, John A. 1977. The Women of Fort Vancouver. Ms. on file, Fort Vancouver National Historic Site, Vancouver, WA.

Merk, Frederick, editor. 1968. *Fur Trade and Empire: George Simpson's Journal 1824–25.* Belknap Press of Harvard University Press. Cambridge, MA.

Miles, Donna. 1995. AAFES Turns 100. *Soldiers.* United States Army, Washington, D.C.

Morrison, Dorothy Nafus. 1998. *Outpost: John McLoughlin and the Far Northwest.* Oregon Historical Society Press: Portland.

Nelson, Peter. 2007. Landscape in the Great Northwest: Investigations of Four Hudson's Bay Company Posts. Ms. on file, Fort Vancouver National Historic Site, Vancouver, WA.

Ott, Jennifer. 2003. "Ruining the Rivers in the Snake Country: The Hudson's Bay Company's Fur Desert Policy. *Oregon Historical Quarterly* 104(2):166–195. Oregon Historical Society: Portland.

Rich, E.E. editor. 1943. *The Letters of John McLoughlin, from Fort Vancouver to the Governor and Committee: Second series, 1839–44.* Champlain Society: Toronto.

Ross, Lester A. 1976. Fort Vancouver, 1829–1960: A historical archeological investigation of the goods imported and manufactured by the Hudson's Bay Company. Ms. on file, Fort Vancouver National Historic Site, Vancouver, WA.

Simon, John Y., editor. 1967. *The Personal Papers of Ulysses S. Grant, Vol. I: 1837–1861.* Southern University Press: Carbondale, IL.

Van Kirk, Sylvia. 1983. *Many Tender Ties: Women in Fur-Trade Society, 1670–1870.* University of Oklahoma Press: Norman.

Wilkes, Charles. 1856. *Narrative of the United States Exploring Expedition During the Years 1838, 1839, 1840, 1841, 1842.* G.P. Putnam & Co.: New York.

Technology

Best, Spencer, editor. 1918. *Monthly Bulletin: Spruce Production Division and Loyal Legion of Loggers and Lumbermen, Vol. 2 No. 3.* Information Section, Spruce Production Division, Bureau of Aircraft Production, U. S. Army: Portland, OR.

Cross, Osborne. 1967. *March of the Regiment of Mounted Riflemen to Oregon in 1849.* Ye Galleon Press: Fairfield, WA.

Delgado, James P. 1993. *The Beaver: First Steamship on the Pacific Coast.* Horsdal & Schubert: Victoria, B.C., Canada.

Erigero, Patricia. 1992. Cultural Landscape Report, Vol. I. Cultural Resources Division, Pacific Northwest Region, National Park Service, Seattle, WA.

Farnham, Thomas J. 1843. *Travels in the Great Western Prairies, the Anahuac and Rocky Mountains, and in the Oregon Territory.* Wiley and Putnam: New York.

Hoffman, J. J. and Lester A. Ross. 1974. Fort Vancouver Excavations VI: Sale Shop & Powder Magazine. Ms. on file, Fort Vancouver National Historic Site, Vancouver, WA.

Hussey, John A. 1970. The Fort Vancouver Farm. Ms. on file, Fort Vancouver National Historic Site, Vancouver, WA.

Hussey, John A. 1976. Historic Structures Report: Historical Data Vol. II. Ms. on file, Fort Vancouver National Historic Site, Vancouver, WA.

Moulton, Gary E., ed. 1990. *The Journals of the Lewis & Clark Expedition, Volume 6, November 2, 1805–March 22, 1806.* University of Nebraska Press: Lincoln.

———. 1991 *The Journals of the Lewis & Clark Expedition, Volume 7, March 22, 1806–June 9, 1806.* University of Nebraska Press: Lincoln.

Rich, E.E. editor. 1941. *The Letters of John McLoughlin, from Fort Vancouver to the Governor and Committee: First series, 1825–38.* Champlain Society: Toronto.

Ross, Lester A. 1976. Fort Vancouver, 1829–1960: A historical archeological investigation of the goods imported and manufactured by the Hudson's Bay Company. Ms. on file, Fort Vancouver National Historic Site, Vancouver, WA.

Ross, Lester A. 1990. Trade Beads from Hudson's Bay

Company Fort Vancouver (1829–1860), Vancouver, Washington. *Beads: Journal of the Society of Bead Researchers* 2:29–68.

Russell, Carl P. 1967. *Firearms, Traps, & Tools of the Mountain Men.* University of New Mexico Press: Albuquerque.

Shine, Gregory P. "An Indispensable Point:" A Historic Resource Study of the Vancouver Ordnance Depot and Arsenal, 1849–1882. Ms. on file, Fort Vancouver National Historic Site, Vancouver, WA.

Sinclair, Donna L. 2004. Part I, "Our Manifest Destiny Bids Fair For Fulfillment:" An Historical Overview of Vancouver Barracks, 1846–1898, with suggestions for further research. Report by the Center for Columbia River History for the National Park Service, Fort Vancouver National Historic Site, Vancouver, WA.

———. 2003. Part Two, The Waking of a Military Town: Vancouver, Washington and the Vancouver National Historic Reserve, 1898–1920. Report by the Center for Columbia River History for the National Park Service, Fort Vancouver National Historic Site, Vancouver, WA.

———. 2005. Part III, Riptide on the Columbia: A Military Community Between the Wars, Vancouver, Washington and the Vancouver Historic Reserve, 1920–1942, with suggestions for further research. Report by the Center for Columbia River History for the National Park Service, Fort Vancouver National Historic Site, Vancouver, WA.

Stevens, Isaac. 1855. Narrative and final report of explorations for a route for a Pacific railroad, near the forty-seventh and forty-ninth parallels of north latitude from St. Paul to Puget Sound. *Reports of explorations and surveys to ascertain the most practicable and economical route for a railroad from the Mississippi River to the Pacific Ocean*, Vol. XII, Book 1. Thomas H Ford: Washington.

Tonsfeldt, Ward. 2003. Spruce Mill Trail Brochure. Edited by Elaine Dorset. Ms. on file, Fort Vancouver National Historic Site, Vancouver, WA.

Wilkes, Charles. 1856. *Narrative of the United States Exploring Expedition During the Years 1838, 1839, 1840, 1841, 1842.* G.P. Putnam & Co.: New York.

Globalization

Beechert, Alice and Edward Beechert. 2005. Hawaiians at Fort Vancouver. Ms. on file, Fort Vancouver National Historic Site, Vancouver, WA.

Dunn, John. 1845. *The Oregon Territory and the British North American Fur Trade.* G. B. Zieber & Co.: Philadelphia.

Giddens, Anthony. 1990. *The Consequences of Modernity.* Polity Press: Cambridge, U. K.

Rich, E.E. editor. 1941. *The Letters of John McLoughlin, from Fort Vancouver to the Governor and Committee: First series, 1825–38.* Champlain Society: Toronto.

Strong, Emory. 1975. The Enigma of the Phoenix Button. *Historical Archaeology* 9:74–80.

Wilkes, Charles. 1856. *Narrative of the United States Exploring Expedition During the Years 1838, 1839, 1840, 1841, 1842.* G.P. Putnam & Co.: New York.

Health

Boyd, Robert T. 1999. *The Coming Spirit of Pestilence: Introduced Infectious Diseases and Population Decline among Northwest Coast Indians, 1774–1874.* University of Washington Press: Seattle.

Carley, Caroline D. 1979. Historical and Archaeological Evidence of Nineteenth Century Fever Epidemics and Medicine at Hudson's Bay Company Fort Vancouver. Master's Thesis, Department of Anthropology, University of Idaho, Moscow.

Rich, E.E. editor. 1941. *The Letters of John McLoughlin, from Fort Vancouver to the Governor and Committee: First series, 1825–38.* Champlain Society: Toronto.

Munnick, Harriet, editor. 1972. *Catholic Church records of the Pacific Northwest: Vancouver, Volumes I and II, and Stellamaris Mission.* Trans. Mikell De Lores Wormell Warner. French Prairie Press: St. Paul, OR.

Tolmie, William Fraser. 1963. *The Journals of William Fraser Tolmie: Physician and Fur Trader.* Mitchell Press Limited: Vancouver, B.C., Canada.

Whitman, Narcissa Prentiss. 1994. *My Journal: 1836.* Ye Galleon Press: Fairfield, WA.

INDEX

Page numbers in *italics* indicate photographs and figures.